A Mad Box of Rain

A Mad Box of Rain

Brian J. Quattlebaum

Published by Brian J. Quattlebaum, 2024.

While every precaution has been taken in the preparation of this book, the publisher assumes no responsibility for errors or omissions, or for damages resulting from the use of the information contained herein.

A MAD BOX OF RAIN

First edition. March 30, 2024.

Copyright © 2024 Brian J. Quattlebaum.

ISBN: 979-8224370528

Written by Brian J. Quattlebaum.

Table of Contents

A Mad Box of Rain 1

Opinion | (so as to spark conversation) 2

Preface 3

Part 1 | My Lost Childhood 4

Chapter 1 | Al-Anon | November 1983 5

Chapter 2 | Run away attempt #1 | Fall 1987 9

Chapter 3 | The beginning | October 1991 14

Chapter 4 | Run away attempt #2 19

Chapter 5 | Busted 23

Chapter 6 | An undisclosed short-term drug treatment center nearby 29

Chapter 7 | First day (I'm not so different as that kid) 33

Chapter 8 | The hook 37

Part 2 41

Chapter 9 | Ride to Second Chance | (Should've been run away attempt #3) | November 1991 42

Chapter 10 | Second Chance intake 43

Chapter 11 | First phase (prior to Talk) 51

Chapter 12 | The Cassidys (Scotty and Jean) 65

Chapter 13 | Friday night rap 72

Chapter 14 | Run away attempt #3 76

Chapter 15 | Sunday (chore day) 82

Chapter 16 | Monday (run day) 83

Chapter 17 | Stuck with nowhere but up to go 85

Chapter 18 | The Key to Willingness | December 1991 88

Chapter 19 | A New Year | January 1992 93

Chapter 20 | Talk & Responsibility 94

Chapter 21 | Second phase (coming home) | March 1992 96

Chapter 22 | The exorcism 102

Chapter 23 | Third phase | June 1992 104

Chapter 24 | Runaway 107

Chapter 25 | Back to school | September 1992 109

Chapter 26 | Fourth phase | October 1992 113

Chapter 27 | Christian music 115

Chapter 28 | The Far Side 117

Chapter 29 | Thanksgiving | November 1992 119

Chapter 30 | Fifth phase | December 1992 121

Chapter 31 | Christmas play | December 1992 123

Chapter 32 | New Year 1993 124

Chapter 33 | Surprising gift | March 1993 126

Chapter 34 | Graduation! | End of May 1993 127

Chapter 35 | Aftercare | Summer 1993 129

Chapter 36 | Chickenpox | July 1993 131

Chapter 37 | Senior fall at Germantown High | Fall 1993 134

Chapter 38 | Christmas 1993 137

Part 3 140

Chapter 39 | New Year 1994 141

Chapter 40 | Back to Collierville High... 142

Chapter 41 | Senior prom 147

Chapter 42 | Pink Floyd 148

Chapter 43 | High-school graduation | June 1994 149

Chapter 44 | Summer before college | 1994.. 150

Chapter 45 | Mississippi State University (Honor's College) | Fall 1994 151

Chapter 47 | The freshman incident | Fall 1994.................................. 154

Chapter 48 | Headed home | Winter 1994/95 157

Chapter 49 | Getting to see Jerry | Spring 1995 159

Chapter 50 | AP Psychology | Summer 1995 161

Chapter 51 | Four years of sobriety | Fall 1995 – Fall 1996............... 162

Chapter 52 | Five years of sobriety | October 1996 164

Chapter 53 | Discovering Oregon | December 1996 167

Chapter 54 | The mysterious illness | January 1997 169

Chapter 55 | My cure | Spring 1997 171

Chapter 56 | The next day | April 1997 173

Chapter 57 | 1997 Alabama Regional Rainbow Gathering | April 1997 174

Chapter 58 | The Quattlebaum Family Reunion (Toad Suck, Arkansas) 177

Chapter 59 | My Oregon Trail | June 1997 180

Chapter 60 | Kansas City breakdown | June 1997 183

Chapter 61 | Lincoln, Nebraska | June 1997 185

Chapter 62 | Windy | June 1997 186

Chapter 63 | Welcome Home | June 1997 187

Chapter 64 | 1997 Oregon National Rainbow Gathering | June 1997 188

Chapter 65 | Ashland, Oregon | July 1997 193

Chapter 66 | Naked hippies on bikes! | 4th of July 1997 196

Chapter 67 | My hippie name | July 1997 197

Chapter 68 | My first bus | July 1997 198

Chapter 69 | The hustle | July 1997 201

Chapter 70 | On the road again | August 1997 203

Chapter 71 | Northern Cali | August 1997 204

Chapter 72 | Southern Cali | August 1997 206

Chapter 73 | Quartzsite, Arizona | August 1997 207

Chapter 74 | Rainbow reunion | August 1997 209

Chapter 75 | Flagstaff, Arizona | September 1997 211

Chapter 76 | Tucson, Arizona | September/October 1997 214

Chapter 77 | Fall Gathering | November 1997 218

Chapter 78 | Winter | December 1997 220

Chapter 79 | The parting (epilogue) | January 1998 224

A Mad Box of Rain

(One man's journey towards self-enlightenment)

by Brian J. Quattlebaum

Cover illustration by Murphy Shaw

Opinion
(so as to spark conversation)

There are, in my opinion, three types of people:

First, there are those that see a worm frying on the hot sidewalk and rescue it by gently picking it up and placing it onto the lawn in a shady area close by.

Second, there are those that see the worm, think about rescuing it, and decide maybe it's better not to rescue it, so they leave it to chance. Of course, the worm fries 99.9% of the time, unless the first type of person happens upon them.

Lastly, there are those people that get delightful and insidious joy out of leaving the worm on the hot, scorching sidewalk. They might even pause to watch. I've witnessed them doing so; me unable to intervene without looking completely foolish and being bullied.

I, the author of this novel, will always rescue that worm. As passively and gently as I can. Unfortunately, because of the madness of my nature, I will also use that same worm as bait for fishing. It's human nature. It's my nature.

Preface

This is an honest recounting of my childhood and teenage years. It covers sensitive subjects such as childhood sexual, physical, emotional, mental, institutional, and substance abuse. It is told in my Southern American internal dark humor voice that has helped me get through these things. Hopefully my story will help you as well.

Part 1
My Lost Childhood

Chapter 1
Al-Anon
November 1983

I had just turned seven when I went to my first Al-Anon meeting in Memphis, Tennessee. Most kids spent their nights and weekends playing games and then headed off to early bedtime. Instead, my parents dragged me to group therapy sessions for loved ones of alcoholics. It wasn't really their fault in my opinion; it wasn't really anyone's fault. It was madness. It just happened.

At the time, my thirteen-year-old brother, who was six years older than me, was extremely creative and got in trouble a lot.

For instance, one afternoon a month prior, he had decided it was a grand idea to steal a whole bottle of vodka from a neighborhood girlfriend's parents' house. He and the girlfriend then decided to drink the entire bottle on the roof of the girl's house, in the middle of the day; getting so drunk that he eventually fell off the roof.

Luckily, it was a one-story house, and he landed on the soft grass and was ok; but the girl's parents were not pleased to find a passed out drunk thirteen-year-old boy on their front lawn. Especially when they found out he stole and drank an entire bottle of their vodka with their daughter.

My poor parents and I, God bless us, came home shortly after to find some very pissed off neighbors wanting nothing more than to give this drunk dumbass boy back to us. They were confused and astounded; we were confused and astounded.

I mostly remember my parents shoveling coffee into him in the downstairs half-bath while he profusely puked into his newly found porcelain god; that cold and brutal god, he, and many others, including myself, have come to know oh so well.

Fast forward one month, and my brother, still thirteen, was in his first short-term drug treatment center in Memphis, Tennessee, and I was having to attend Al-Anon meetings. My parents weren't rich, they were middle class at best, but they had good health insurance.

My mom was a Certified Pediatric Nurse who worked at a large children's medical center in downtown Memphis, mainly post-ICU and graveyard shifts. She's made a difference in countless children's lives. No matter their background or monetary status.

My father worked for a computer processing giant (one of the first). He liked math, had a master's degree in computer science, and he was good at programming Basic. He was a good man but stubborn as a bull at the time.

Both of my parents worked hard and had a profound impact on my ability and willingness to achieve "an honest day's pay for an honest day's work." They were Southern Christian parents just trying to raise their two boys the best they could.

My parents couldn't really understand why this madness with my brother was happening to them. They tried their best to be good parents. I must believe that the community tried its best.

So, here I sat at seven years old in 1983 at an Al-Anon meeting held inside some random church in Memphis with a bunch of strangers. My parents and I were gathered with about twenty other folks in a large circle of metal folding chairs, hearing the Serenity Prayer for the first time, and very confused about what the hell was going on.

Now, for those that don't know, the Serenity Prayer is a mantra popularized by Alcoholics Anonymous and other support groups. The short and simple version says: "God grant me the serenity to accept the things I cannot change, courage to change the things I can, and the wisdom to know the difference." I didn't know it at the time, but that mantra would become a recurring theme in my life; whether I liked it or not. I still get nauseous every time I see that prayer hanging on a wall.

If I was lucky on those nights at various support group meetings, the groups would be split between siblings and parents. I was rarely that lucky. I usually had to sit with the adults and hear their stories.

This would be the first time I thought about telling my terrible "secret" to anyone but was too scared to do so. I wish I had; my life may have ended up being a little easier for me. I hid my secret from everyone for another nine years.

I, instead, continued to suffer in silence while going to various support group sessions for dependents, most of the time run by private institutions, until it was my turn to be labeled "the bad kid."

I lived at the time in a small town thirty minutes east of Memphis, called Collierville, Tennessee. My brother and I were very bored in a small town and tended to get into trouble a lot. Our childhood path was laid out before us: try to creatively stay busy, but constantly end up bored. Maybe God wanted us to be bored, so we could be more creative?

I'll try to keep this brief, but when I said earlier that we were Southern Christian, I mean we were part of a very small church's congregation in Collierville called Greenhill's Baptist in the early 1980s. Greenhill's had a total congregation of around 100 people. Most of the Collierville residents went to the larger First Baptist across town instead.

My dad was in the church choir, as was I, until I started puberty. My family and I were regular church goers and, when we weren't in family therapy or Al-Anon meetings, we went to church twice on Sundays and then to mid-week Bible school every Wednesday night.

I tried my best to stay busy in Collierville and have an innocent childhood. However, thanks to a combination of what passed for "good" parenting advice at the time (spawned by the Tough Love movement, the war on drugs, church, and therapists), I was the only other young kid I knew who got to learn instead about the difference between pills on my nights and weekends.

Pop Quiz: who here has ever been a student in their second grade Say No to Drugs program when they knew more about the drugs than the local cop assigned to teach us? Answer: me.

To top it all off, I also had my huge secret that was eating me from the inside out. I wasn't feeling all too jolly.

Chapter 2
Run away attempt #1
Fall 1987

I was nine the first time I ran away. My parents hadn't really done anything to deserve it. I just couldn't stand reality due to so much repressed and built-up pain and embarrassment over my secret.

I remember I used to daydream during school, as early as kindergarten, about just getting up and bolting out the classroom door, skipping merrily across the neighboring field while all the students and teachers watched from the classroom windows. Where to, I don't know. Just away.

I wasn't that brazen. Instead, I just decided not to catch the school bus in the morning. I didn't like the heaping pile of lemons that life had dumped upon my life. I was convinced in my head that I was going away where everything would magically be better. Providence would favor me; I was sure of it.

I decided that morning that I was going to walk to my brother's friend's house twenty miles away. I had no clue if they were home. My brother was no longer living at home by then. A few years prior though, he had stolen my parents' car one night and driven us to his friend's house. I had the impression that night that his friend had a cool family. Funny how memories stick with us at that age.

I did it right, too. I had a pillowcase with a change of clothes in it tied around a stick and carried over my shoulder. Hobo-style.

So, my nine-year-old self ended up walking in the rural Tennessee woods alongside a two-lane country road most of the way. To this day

I am impressed by how far I got; fifteen of those twenty miles. I walked all morning and most of the early afternoon.

I got caught when I ventured into a small convenience store along the way. The lady working at the counter had sense enough to realize I wasn't old enough to be out of school and called the police shortly after I left. I dunno, maybe my hobo sack had given me away?

A Shelby County Sheriff's car eventually pulled up alongside me on the road, and a lone male deputy exited the car. He walked up and asked me in a thick southern voice: "son, why aren't you in school?"

At that point, I was busted, so I passionately explained to him that I was running away. He gently laughed and then drove me to the Collierville police station; me sitting in the front passenger seat and getting to play with the radar and siren on the way back.

My parents came home from work that afternoon and did not find me there as they expected. Instead, very worried, they checked their answering machine and found the Collierville police on it, letting them know where I was. They immediately came to the police station and got me. I don't remember them being too upset, just extremely concerned.

I was taken to a family therapist by my parents as soon as possible after my first run away attempt. I remember sitting alone outside of a therapist's office for a long time, playing a board game by myself in the waiting room while my parents talked in private with the therapist. I would find out later from my parents, when I was an adult, that what they were discussing was that they thought something was wrong but couldn't get "my secret" out of me. Maybe the therapist could?

My parents came out of the therapist's office, and the therapist gestured for me to follow her in. I didn't jell with her to say the least. Something about her immediate coldness and condescension did not make me feel like opening up at all.

Towards the end of the therapy session, I could tell the therapist was getting flustered. She started saying things like "Brian, quit playing games. You're playing games with me, your parents, and everyone else in your life. Life is not a game. Quit playing games," repeating the same thing for several minutes.

It didn't work. I remained silent. Giving up, she ushered me out to the lobby where I got to go back to my board game, and my parents could go in and talk about me again. At least I had a game to occupy my time with.

For the next several years, my parents would continue to drag me to therapists, I would continue to hide my secret, and my real problems would never be addressed.

I was a stuffed-up, angry little boy who loved to escape on my Nintendo game console and was grateful for the limited time I got to play with my friends at church. I always made honor roll and rarely got in trouble at school.

One night when I was fourteen and listening to my boombox cassette radio alone in my room, trying to make a favorite mixed-tape, I made a mental and emotional breakthrough. I immediately pulled myself out of a spiraling depression by discovering the Grateful Dead. This was when I first heard the band perform a live show, on a Memphis station called Rock 103. It was a repeat of a recent Chicago show.

It was the greatest, most positive, most uplifting, real lyrics and music I had ever experienced. The music was uplifting to me and very complex. It spoke to my soul, and it reminded me of a lot of the gospel and bluegrass music my father loved. So, naturally, I started following the music. It became poetry to me. I fell in love with Robert Hunter's lyrics and the Grateful Dead. I started writing poetry at that age because of it. I instantly became a Deadhead that night.

I remember reading a book about the band saying something along the lines that it was a symbiotic circle, taking care of one's own family to create more with that family than one could do solely on their own. The audience was part of the band and live music being created; thus, the audience participated in the creation of the music. We were all musicians; we were all dancers. Everyone was grateful for everyone. I dug that.

Shortly after, while a freshman in high school, I met another, older, Deadhead who was a junior. He had older friends who were going to the Grateful Dead shows. This gave him a steady supply of two things: pure LSD acid inside of sugar cubes and marijuana. He also had a car.

So, over the summer between my freshman and sophomore year at Collierville High School, I got a lot cooler in my opinion. I enjoyed eating the sugar cubes by myself in my bedroom and staying up most of the night watching MTV while tripping balls. I found that the psychedelics eased my childhood trauma. I had never felt happier in my life.

The same friend also gave me a glow-in-the-dark neon green puff paint bottle. It was clear and plastic. It would become my blankie for a short while.

I would eat an LSD infused sugar cube at night alone in my bedroom in the dark and wait for my visuals to kick in while watching MTV. I would then charge the luminescent paint of the puff paint bottle with a bedside lamp and throw it across the room while lying on my bed, immediately losing myself giggling at the lovely after trails that glowed across the room like a neon green rainbow. After the visual trailing of the bottle eventually died, I'd get up the courage to go across my bedroom and retrieve my puff paint bottle. Charging and then throwing it again.

I tried doing psychedelics in a social setting once or twice during this time. I did not like it and became too paranoid. There was way too much internal stuff going on with me that I needed to process privately. I always tried to get home to my bedroom as quickly as possible.

Now, this is where the story gets a little sadder. However, it's not the typical sad, romanticized story one hears played out in Hollywood and in most people's heads. The key difference being that I, and a large portion of teenager's institutionalized at that time, hadn't really done anything illegal except experiment with alcohol and drugs.

I wasn't a thief. I wasn't a thug. I wasn't a murderer. I hadn't broken any consequential laws. I hadn't been arrested. I hadn't been tried, judged, or sentenced by any real authority.

I eventually lost many friends I met through treatment and support groups due to suicide, or the ever-popular Memphis Christian version "suicide by cop" (calling the police to your place and coming out with a gun raised so they would shoot you dead).

I guess the best thing I can say is that at least I'm still alive and able to tell my story. Maybe it will touch and dissuade some parents who are thinking about putting their child into a long-term drug treatment center.

Brainwashing is a real thing. It has irreparable effects. It is insidious and the opposite of love. I have severe Obsessive-Compulsive Disorder, General Anxiety Disorder, recurrent Major Depressive Disorder, and a few other fancy-sounding mental disorders I must be constantly treated for because of the following true story. My disorders are never going to go away; the best I can hope for is being able to manage them well enough that I can somewhat function in society. Please don't intentionally do this to your children.

Chapter 3
The beginning
October 1991

The end of my freedom started one Friday night after school at the beginning of October 1991. I had just turned fifteen a week earlier and had a small, street legal motorcycle that I would putter around Collierville on. I loved doing nothing more at the time than riding my motorcycle around town. I felt so free.

I was high on that same feeling that night, but completely sober, while riding my motorcycle to my friend's house after the high school football game. His parents were out-of-town. Party!

By this time, I was a sophomore in high school who had a motorcycle and a huge crush on my friend's sister, whose house I was going to. So, wanting to be cool, I decided to stop alone at a local apartment complex of some friends to try and buy some marijuana to bring to the party and impress her.

Now, at this point, I had smoked a little marijuana. When I say a little, I mean a couple of times, at most, with older school friends. It was hard to get back then at that age. Probably still is, seeing that it's Collierville, Tennessee. However, the few times I had previously smoked marijuana as a teen resulted in me having a great time laughing and chilling with my friends. The horror.

So, here I am, fifteen, puttering down the Collierville streets on a fall Friday night on my motorcycle, completely sober, riding to these apartments where my friend had gotten marijuana from a week prior. I pulled up, got off my bike, and said in a discrete voice to a couple of the older guys in the parking lot that I knew from before, "Howdy, y'all remember me from the other day, I was with my friend. I was wondering if y'all had any dope I could get?" Yes, I said the word "dope."

See, as brilliant as I thought I was at street slang at the time, I still got "dope" and "pot" mixed up. Maybe I was just nervous. It was 1991, I was fifteen, and I had no real clue what I was doing.

They all looked at each other, and one replied with a serious look on his face (which briefly puzzled me at the time), "ya, but it's going to take about thirty minutes and it's going to cost a lot." I replied, "ya, sure, I'll wait."

I remember thinking to myself that it was weird that they didn't have any marijuana with them or close by. I am certain they were thinking to themselves that it was weird this scrawny dumbass tall kid was asking for "dope." Fun times.

So, I waited in the parking lot of the complex while sitting on a curb and staring patiently at the asphalt. They returned about forty-five minutes later. I handed them the money, and they handed me a small clear plastic bag of crack cocaine rocks. My jaw hit the pavement, and I said, "Is this crack?!?" They replied back, "ya, you said you wanted dope."

It didn't take long for it to dawn on all of us, while standing under the parking lot lights that night, that what I had meant earlier was "pot," "weed," "marijuana flower"; not "dope."

They laughed hard, basically calling me a scrawny dumbass kid, and said they'd had weed on them since the beginning, but I'd have to wait because they'd left it back in the apartment. Also, it would cost more money.

Since that was the last of my cash, I politely declined and rode away on my motorcycle with the bag of crack rocks to my friend's party. Somehow, I lost the baggie along the way. Since my friends weren't really the crack cocaine crowd, I must have decided to do a smart thing and toss it into a roadside ditch.

Honestly, I don't remember how I got rid of it, but I didn't have the crack when I arrived, and we fortunately didn't use it. So, I arrived on my motorcycle, fashionably late, with no marijuana, but also luckily, no crack cocaine.

There were about thirty high school kids there, no adults, and the only thing we had to drink were several boxes of cheap white wine in the fridge. My inexperience with the wine resulted in me getting a little excited and drinking two Solo cups full in under an hour. The chilled wine tasted like candy to me.

Now, if you've ever had a couple of Solo cups of boxed wine while fifteen years old within a one-hour time span, you know - I was torn up from the floor up. Swillyier than a fruit tree. I certainly was in no shape to drive my motorcycle home. So, I did the smart thing and called home to see if I could spend the night at my friend's house.

Unfortunately, my dad answered the phone. He was immediately suspicious and told me to come home a.s.a.p. I said I couldn't, hung up, and walked off to go talk with some friends. I somehow ended up on my friend's parents' bed shortly after and passed out, missing the rest of the party.

That was the last alcohol that I would ingest for five years. I didn't smoke marijuana again for five years either. I was to become a completely sober teen from age fifteen to twenty, minus the drugs the doctor prescribed for me at a short-term drug treatment center.

I woke up the next morning with a splitting headache and a few brave souls left at the house. They were quick to tell me that my motorcycle was gone.

Apparently, my dad had called the house back after I hung up on him and was able to convince the gullible teen on the other end to give out the address. My dad then came to the house, and, after no one said where I was, he convinced a couple of the teens to help him load my motorcycle onto the bed of his truck, driving away in the middle of the night with it.

Thanks a lot, guys. I get it though. My dad was a bullish dick and usually got his way. Also, he bought the motorcycle for me, so I still feel he had the right to do it, at least according to his scruples. I do wish he'd been more understanding at the time and seen that I had actually made the responsible choice by not trying to drive my motorcycle home drunk.

Luckily, my friend's sister, whom I had a huge crush on, was willing to give me a ride back to my house in her car that following morning. I don't remember much, but according to her, we had a nice conversation the night before while I was drunk. She had taken pity on me and let me sleep in their parents' bed.

That was encouraging. Nothing physical between us had happened, but at least I didn't come off as a total drunk dumbass. Or she was just being nice to me. Who knows? I never got the chance to find out.

I arrived home around ten o'clock the next morning and found my dad in the living room watching television in his recliner. My dad was never a man of many words, so, in the shortest way possible, he explained to me that my motorcycle was locked up in the garage. I was grounded, indefinitely, and they had already contacted the emergency family crisis line through his insurance to get a therapist appointment that Tuesday.

My parents were convinced that I was an alcoholic and drug addict, just like my brother, and needed professional help.

I was floored. This was the first time that I had been "caught" doing anything like this. I tried my best to explain how I was just trying to do the right thing by calling them, letting them know where I was, and not driving home; but my dad wasn't listening to it.

I opened the garage door and looked out. Sure enough, he had chained up my motorcycle frame to the wheels and padlocked it all together.

Chapter 4
Run away attempt #2

I spent the rest of Saturday and all day Sunday in my bedroom, avoiding my parents as much as possible. I was dumbfounded, and I was stewing in my head, alone. A deep, desperate, dark depression had swallowed me whole. I felt trapped and needed to escape. I would have given anything to escape that feeling. I almost gave everything by ending my story, alone, in my bedroom. Music, mainly the Grateful Dead and Beastie Boys, came to the rescue again. Thank you, musicians, for saving my life so many times.

Come Monday morning, I had devised an ingenious plan. I still had my motorcycle keys in my possession, so I waited until my parents left for work, and, instead of going to school, I called the local locksmith in the Yellow Pages. I calmly explained on the phone that my parents had accidentally left for work with the key to my motorcycle chain, it was locked because we were afraid it'd get stolen, and that I needed it unlocked so I could get to school. He somehow bought it.

When he arrived, he asked for my license in my parents' garage, and I happily gave it to him. I then told him before he started that I didn't have any money on me. But, if he unlocked my motorcycle, he could follow me back to the pawn store while I pawned my fifteen or so Nintendo games (which I showed him in my backpack) that I had been saving up through birthday cash over the years. I was done with them. He could keep my license in the meantime as collateral.

He hesitated for a second, but then, I don't know, out of a stroke of some sort of luck, he unlocked my motorcycle.

I then rode to the pawn store, the locksmith following, pawning my game cartridges for around $3 each. I paid the locksmith $20, and then rode off, quickly booking it out of Collierville and across the state line into Mississippi. Next stop, the Grateful Dead concert in Atlanta, Georgia.

I had no clue exactly when the concert was, or how much it would cost to get there, but I had heard my friends talking about it. I was pretty sure it was happening that next weekend. So, down Highway 72 I rolled on my small ass (125 cc engine) Suzuki motorcycle that surprisingly would smoothly top out at 75 mph.

I made it as far as Corinth, Mississippi, which was 70 miles away, stopping along the way to eat lunch at a roadside diner. When I reached Corinth and was running low on gas, I suddenly realized that I didn't have a lot of options. I had $20 in my pocket and was starving, with no place to stay.

It was an early cold and rainy afternoon, and I realized it was only going to get darker, wetter, and colder. So, I pulled my motorcycle up to the nearest motel parking lot to stop and think. What was I going to do?

Without thinking too much about it, I was barely fifteen after all, I went inside the inn and asked the desk manager if they had any jobs I could do for a couple of hours that night to get a free room. They were desolately empty. The middle-aged male behind the desk looked me up and down, and then asked in his most Southern and commanding voice "are you eighteen? "

At fifteen, I was a scrawny lad, but I had a few things going for me. I was 6'3", had an earring in my left ear, and a constant five o'clock shadow on my face. I could easily pass for nineteen. So, I lied and said, "yes." He asked if I had any identification, and I lied and said "no." I told him that

I had lost my wallet and was heading to my folk's house in Memphis. I was low on cash and didn't want to sleep outside.

God only knows what was going through that managers head, but bless him, he told me "Yes, we have some spots on the lobby carpet that need scrubbing." He then handed me the cleaning supplies, showed me the spots, and demonstrated what to do. I spent the next two hours scrubbing those spots with zeal, glee, and gratitude.

When he deemed I was done, he handed me the key to my room and said he wanted me gone by tomorrow morning. I thanked him from the bottom of my heart, said a silent prayer that he bought some of my bullshit and wouldn't call the cops, and walked out to my motorcycle.

I drove around to the motel room and checked it out. A single queen, with MTV, not bad. It was while I was sitting there on the motel bed, watching a Naughty by Nature rap video on MTV, that it dawned on my small brain, completely, my unfortunate situation. I had $20 left and an empty tank of gas. That was a problem. That would barely get me to Atlanta.

I went to the gas station, now around $10 left. I wasn't a genius, but I finally started doing the math, which included food and shelter, and realized I was in trouble. No way I was going to make it to Atlanta without more money.

While at the gas station contemplating life, I looked over across the street, saw a bowling alley and thought "man, I bet they have cheap hotdogs." I drove over, and sure enough, they not only had a cheap hotdog but also a cheap cigarette vending machine. Hey, necessities, right?

That night in Corinth there wasn't shat to do other than hang out at the bowling alley and smoke cigarettes. But, since it was a Monday night, it was dead. I quickly rode back to my motel room to watch MTV and try to hatch a plan.

I couldn't hatch one. I was fucked. I needed more money to make it to Atlanta.

So, the next morning I decided that, since I had enough money to return to Collierville, I could go back and maybe my best friend would loan me a little bit of cash.

Certainly, my best friend would be understanding and give me some of his savings so I could make it to the Atlanta concert and escape? Right? Well, I never got the chance to find out.

Chapter 5
Busted

I was pulled over by the Collierville police as soon as I crossed over the Mississippi state line and back into Collierville that morning. This guy was hiding behind a billboard trying to catch speeders crossing the state line. He saw my motorcycle, remembered seeing it at the high school parking lot, put one and one together, and pulled me over. His first words were very reminiscent of the officer who busted me the last time I ran away, "Why aren't you in school?" His tone was much harsher.

I told him I was sick, and this dick cuffed me, searched me, and stuffed me in the back of the cop car. I had nothing on me. I wasn't using drugs; I couldn't afford them or easily find them even if I wanted to.

I don't know; maybe the "Quattlebaum" name had gotten a bad rep in Collierville because of my brother. I can't swear to this, but I believe he mentioned my brother's name. Luckily, he didn't shoot, unnecessarily restrain, choke, or tase me. I am very grateful for that. I did, however, get "Bushed," (George Bush, Sr's continuation of Ronald Reagan's "war on drugs"), and also got a big ole helping of "Tough Love." I wish that cop would have been a lot cooler and brought me back to school instead.

My parents arrived at the Collierville police station and picked me up again. This time with me in a holding cell, six years after my first runaway experience. They had tried to report me missing to the police the night before when they came home, however, the Collierville police would not take a report until that next day. They hadn't gone back to work and were worried sick, but they were happy I was alive and safe.

The next time I saw my motorcycle was a few months later when I found out my dad had sold it to the next-door neighbor's kid. I got to watch the kid drive it every now and then for several years after that. He seemed to enjoy it.

The ride home with my parents was deafeningly silent. I immediately went back to my bedroom, knowing I had an appointment with a therapist the next day.

Later that night, my favorite church counselor, and one of my favorite people of all time, Mr. Ed, came over to the house to talk with me in private at my parents' insistence. God, I will forever love that man and his positive impact he had on me while at the Methodist church. He really did try and care.

Mr. Ed told me that he couldn't really relate to drug and alcohol problems, but he confided that, when he was in the Vietnam War, or maybe right after, one of his squad mates had gotten addicted to heroin. He said it was devastating to his whole squad. I didn't know what to say.

Mr. Ed was the caring sort that really tried. He hugged me, we said our goodbyes, and I went to the therapist the next day, motivated to do better.

That next morning, I took the thirty-minute drive into Memphis with my mom; my dad not able to get off work. We met a therapist in her office. I don't know what her degrees and qualifications were, but she was covered by our health insurance.

The therapist pulled my mother in privately first. I sat in the waiting room, which at this point was worse than sitting in a dentist's office. There was nothing worthy of reading, so I just stared at the artwork on the walls. I remember sad sunflower paintings for some reason.

The wait was painful. My mom eventually came out, crying, and I was called in. The therapist's demeanor could best be described as ice cold.

I was 80% honest with the therapist. I didn't mention my secret. I was scared and taking that shit to the grave with me. I also certainly didn't share with her that creative music was about the only thing that helped me multitask and survive in this real world.

In hindsight, it probably would have been a good thing to share, at that only session we would ever have, the entire truth. Might have saved me a heap of trouble. At the time, I didn't fully understand my privacy rights.

I have to hope she wouldn't have sent me where she did and maybe would have had a little more compassion for me if she had known the full story. Unfortunately, I'm not sure she cared. Damned if I do, damned if I don't.

I instead played it safe and answered her questions as truthfully as I could. First, I explained that I had tried marijuana a couple of times with some friends, and we had just chilled and had a good, humorous time hanging out. Then I said that I drank alcohol with my friends on a few occasions, once alone, in a ditch by my house. My friend and I had gotten a bottle of Jack Daniel's whiskey that we stashed at the ditch that previous summer.

My friends and I slowly suckled on that bottle of whiskey. Two swigs each, and we were all good and buzzed; trying our hardest to stay balanced while hiding on the muddy dirt side of a ditch so as not to fall into the shallow, clay bottomed water below.

I also admitted to that cold lady, whom I was completely terrified of, that I had tried LSD and psychedelic mushrooms a few times as well, mainly alone, and that was it. Probably stupid of me, I know. I was just trying to hide my other secret by using drugs as a convenient distraction. I chose poorly.

Unfortunately for me as well, I was probably wearing a tie-die or Grateful Dead t-shirt at the time. If it was a tie-die, unknown to my therapist, my mom had helped me make it. My mom understood the craft at the time and saw how passionate I became when I first discovered them and how to make them. I loved the bi-lateral effect of stitching in the design and getting a mirror image in the folds. It reminded me of a fractal. To be able to experience and make that seemed pretty cool to me, even at a young age.

I certainly wasn't a "bad" kid. The worst thing I had ever done was punch a boy square in the nose in the fifth grade for skipping in front of me, and a lot of other people, in the water fountain line during break outside of our classroom. I know I gave him sufficient warning, and his response was, "yea, so, what are you going to do about it."

I stupidly decided to keep it real and, even though I got the lick in, shit went wrong fast. Our teacher quickly intervened and wanted to know why I had hit him square in his nose, causing him to fall down. I explained, but she didn't care. I had escalated it to physical violence. When class resumed, she assigned busy work to the kids and asked me and the kid I had punched in the nose to join her in the hallway.

My fifth-grade teacher brought her favorite paddle, Dr. Pepper, with her. It was one of her three corporal punishment instruments that she had previously described in detail our first day of class. Her husband, an amateur wood craftsman, had helped her devise them. She also told us that she had mouse traps set in her purse, and that, if any of us got hurt by them, it was legally our fault.

The first of three instruments of wrath she had was called "Mr. Blue." It was approximately eight 6" blue rulers taped together with three rows of masking tape wrapping it into a tight bundle. If a student was unfortunate and did something stupid in class that she deemed worthy of punishment, such as answering a question wrong, she would tell you that Mr. Blue needed to intervene. She would then demand that you hold your left hand out on the desk in front of you while she whacked the back of it several times with Mr. Blue. If you flinched by moving your hand, she would then start level two of the three levels of corporal punishment.

Level two was to be paddled by a 12" long wooden paddle that her husband had made for her. It was flat and relatively light. It stung but didn't actually welp the skin. However, you were paddled in front of the entire class. It was extremely embarrassing but rarely physically hurt for more than five to ten minutes.

Level three, the final level of her punishment before being marched down to the principal in an emotional turmoil of madness, was her husband's and her's favorite creative instrument of destruction. The monstrosity was called "Dr. Pepper" and was an 18" long wooden paddle drilled with multiple holes. The holes were there to overcome as much wind resistance as possible whilst maintaining structural integrity and producing maximum sting and burn to its victims. The handle was wrapped in several layers of masking tape to help provide comfort to its bearer. It usually left welts.

Woe be the kid that didn't say they were sorry while being smacked with the Dr. Pepper paddle outside of the classroom in the hallway. She would smack us degenerates, privately, in the hall as many times as she energetically could. See? I could get my private catholic education at my very public school. Equity for all.

That was the harshest occasion when I physically acted out in school. I understood at the time that physically acting out all of the time would make me a bully. I tried my hardest not to bully any other kids and treated them with love and respect. Seemed the right thing to do.

Back 'round to the not so loving session I was having with this therapist. Instead of explaining some of my past with my therapist, I didn't open up to her, and she quickly ushered me out of her office, calling my mom back in. A little while later, I was called back into her office. The therapist, surely seeing my parents had health insurance that could afford it, diagnosed me the same as my older brother: a teenage alcoholic and drug addict who had the potential of becoming a full-fledge terror on society. Her professional advice: admit me to a short-term drug treatment center that catered to teens as soon as possible.

I remember on the ride home that my mom was sobbing while driving the car, barely able to stay on the road. She kept repeating, "why both of my boys?" out loud, to me, the steering wheel, and I assume, God.

Chapter 6

An undisclosed short-term drug treatment center nearby

Next day (seriously, that fast), I was being admitted by my parents into a short-term drug-treatment center fifteen miles away. Basically, in this author's brief, humble opinion, it was a one-story sprawling brick and window fortress with multiple outstretched arms protruding from the center.

All of the landscape was neatly manicured around a one-acre radius surrounding the fortress. Outside of that, lots of woods. Lots and lots of dark, shaded woods. Woods filled with large oak trees wrapped in poison ivy, oak, and sumac. Oh, also, snakes. Roll the dice on which one you want to stumble into. Not the kind of woods that you wanted to go hiking in off-trail. Nature is a real thing. I humbly advise you to respect it if you ever visit the Mid-South.

As I walked with my parents from our car across a large, paved, and mainly vacant parking lot into this cold, brick and tinted storefront window structure, my heart sank, dumbfounded by the stark bleakness of it all. Quietly nestled into the woods near Memphis, this sprawling monstrosity was the opposite of a comfy Hobbit cave to say the least.

Through the cold double glass doors and into the lobby with my parents I went. There was an older lady there who looked up at us, took our names, and then asked us to wait. We sat patiently in the lobby. About ten minutes later a large gentleman in a white coat came in and demanded I follow him, alone.

The male orderly led me to a small room near the lobby, made me remove my Playboy Bunny loop earring in my left ear that I'd gotten at the mall (I was a virgin rebel back then, what can I say), strip down to my undies, and put on hospital garments; my new "in" look.

Now, I'd seen "One Flew Over the Cuckoo's Nest" previously that summer on censored television. I, even at that age, knew I was fucked. I was really, truly fucked.

The orderly then guided me through security doors after I'd been searched, stripped, and re-branded by him. I was escorted through a long main hallway and eventually ended up in the "under-18" wing.

The under-18 side of the center was locked down in its own wing. That wing was divided into two main patient groups: mental behavior and drug addiction. These two groups were divided by a large corridor, about ten rooms on each side, two beds and a full bathroom to a room. We all shared a common area and access to group rooms for raps (group therapy). There were about fifteen of us kids there at that time, but the place could have easily held many more.

I was taken to my room and told my clothes and necessities my parents had packed in a suitcase would be brought to me later. The other kids were in group raps at that time, but I wasn't allowed to attend the raps the first day and was ordered to stay in my room instead. So, I just stayed in my room, sitting on the edge of my bed with absolutely nothing to do. An orderly eventually brought me supper from the treatment center's on-site cafeteria.

I remember being so bored that I pulled a staple out of one of the only booklets in the room so I could put it into my pierced ear for a few minutes. I thought that maybe if I kept doing it every day for the next thirty days, it wouldn't close back up before I got back out of treatment. Priorities, right?

My roommate came in later after his nightly group raps. He was a year older and seemed cool. He was leaving later that week due to completing the drug treatment center's "program" in a month. I remember him telling me, "Beware of Second Chance – it is long-term." I wish I'd processed and understood what he was trying to tell me at the time.

I slept that night on the first of many uncomfortable beds for the first of many uncomfortable nights.

Now, what happened that first night was alarming to say the least. What I really want to stress to the reader's senses is how utterly terrifying it is to the auditory and nervous system to hear screaming while one is trying to sleep at night. It's especially alarming when the person screaming and wailing is a twelve-year-old kid, and there's nothing you can do about it.

This kid was on the behavioral children's side, just six to eight feet across the wide corridor. I would find out later, through group raps, that he had been badly sexually and physically abused by a family member. He had been physically acting out consistently on a daily and nightly basis ever since. He'd been admitted several weeks before.

The boy's abuser was his mom's stepfather who was currently waiting at home for him whenever he got out. Since nothing could be proved, the abuser was never arrested. The boy's mom didn't believe the kid either, hence why he was in the behavioral treatment center. It was the boy's word against the abuser's word, an adult. I'd been acting like a trapped raving animal as well if I were in his shoes.

When things finally fell quiet that night, I felt what a parent feels when their child finally goes silent and falls asleep – grateful and relieved.

Unfortunately, the next morning I found out what had happened to make the twelve-year-old boy quiet in the middle of the night. See, the drug treatment center's answer to the terrifying emotional and mental pain this child was going through was to not believe him and have orderlies strap him to a stretcher, inject him by needle in the arm with an instantly acting sedative, and wheel him away down the corridor into a separate room to leave him.

The first of many times that I witnessed this was the next morning when it happened again before breakfast. I got to watch it from my room across the hall. It quickly dawned on me why the kid had gone so quiet the night before. I suddenly didn't feel so grateful and relieved whenever the quiet would come after that.

Chapter 7
First day (I'm not so different as that kid)

After breakfast in the treatment center's cafeteria, corralled by orderlies with around fifteen kids who were zonked out on sedatives, I ventured into my first rap group. We sat in a circle and talked about our past drug experiences and feelings to the therapist leading the rap. Not very exciting unless someone decided to embellish.

Sometimes the raps would be split between the behavioral health patients and the addiction patients. I believe it mimicked the adult side. A therapist would lead it (rarely ever a doctor), and we kids would talk while sitting in a circle. Taking turns sharing.

I was truthful, but not honest, when it came my turn to share. I may have enriched the truth a slight bit to impress the other kids, but no outright lies. Even though I still couldn't talk about my secret, I was able to talk a little bit about my feelings. Since I was in the drug and alcohol group of kids, I'm sure the therapist immediately attached my feelings to substance abuse. I didn't give him much else to work with.

After morning rap, we went to the gym to exercise. The drug treatment center had a nice little gymnasium with a rubber court where they taught aerobics and karate, alternating daily, for one hour throughout the week.

Now, this next bit was a little shocking to me. I had been taking Taekwondo since I was ten years old. I was determined that no one was going to abuse me or those I cared about again if I could physically do something about it. I had already achieved my first black belt rank, which I lost due to inactivity but later reclaimed when I was free from my bonds, and I had seriously dabbled in Aikido. I loved the spiritual aspect of Aikido. I'm not going to say I was a badass, but I knew what was going on.

The gym instructor was a Japanese Karate black belt instructor. Yes, he was white and not Japanese. Kind of reminded me of a Southern Steven Seagal. He was the authority, right?

After I explained to the instructor my previous training experience, he became a serious dick in my opinion. He was incredibly sure that the way I was punching wasn't right. He preceded to chide me in front of the whole class on how wrong my training was after I told him my "styles" and why it was that way.

Afterwards, I solemnly walked back, us being guided in a single file line by the orderlies down the hallway to morning group raps. My head hung low. I felt humiliated. I didn't understand at the time that sometimes haters gonna hate. Usually that hate comes from misperceptions that keep repeating themselves into a cycle of abuse. Not cool.

Sometime that afternoon, I can't remember exactly when, one of the larger male orderlies pushed me from behind while I was walking into my room. My anger took over; I couldn't help it. I turned around and told him in a very loud voice to never fucking touch me again.

Suddenly there were three orderlies in my room, one with a straitjacket. Yea, a real freaking straitjacket. They gave me two options: either put on the straitjacket, or they were going to strap me to a gurney and sedate me. I opted for the straitjacket; I didn't want to get strapped to a stretcher and shot up with a needle like that other kid.

In hindsight, I probably could have taken on all three of the orderlies. But then, where was I going to go? Every exit was locked with a delayed alarm. I was trapped. I complied.

After they strapped me into the straitjacket, the orderlies walked me down the corridor to the same small room I had seen them wheel the twelve-year-old boy's stretcher into earlier that morning. It was around 8'x8' and all white, all padded. Everywhere. Ceiling, floor, walls. All white, buttoned, padded squares.

They threw me in and locked the door.

I remember a bright light in the room, but to this day I have no idea where it was coming from. I'm pretty sure I was in that room for more than twelve hours, but who knows for sure?

I do remember that at one point a nurse came into the room and made me swallow two pills that were in a small paper cup, followed by another small cup with water. I would later find out that the pill was called Ativan (lorazepam) and turned me into a zombie if taken in large doses. Especially since I was still a twig of a kid.

This would be the last time I'd be coherent and off drugs for the next twenty-eight days. From then on, for the next few weeks while I was at the short-term drug treatment center, I was a pale, scrawny zombie on prescribed drugs. It was fucking madness.

Now, I wouldn't blame anyone reading this for thinking that I might have an intellectual problem. Hell, even I was thinking it after being straitjacketed, but fortunately that was not the case. I had made honor roll my whole life without really trying, but maybe that was just dumb luck. Luckily, the treatment center decided to test my intelligence that first week.

A day or so after this horrible ordeal, I was escorted to the barber. They buzzed away my medium-length hair. Afterwards, the orderlies took me into a side-room. When I entered, there sat a guy, probably in his mid-thirties, in the small and cramped space. He was nicely dressed and directed a genuine smile of sympathy my way. He told me to sit across from him at a table and asked the orderlies to leave.

The guy introduced himself and said he was hired by the treatment center to do Intelligence Quotient (IQ) tests on the patients here. He then administered a bunch of tests to me for several hours, mainly consisting of puzzles and questions, sometimes by solving a physical puzzle in front of him while being timed. Other times he would ask a series of random questions or have me look at flash cards. I remember enjoying it, the test was fun.

The next day, I was pulled into the side room again by orderlies, and the same guy was there. He wanted to share my results and gave me my number, 145. Even while drugged, I ranked higher than "above average" for someone my age. So, I wasn't of low intelligence. That was a relief.

Chapter 8
The hook

One of the few things I remember about the short-term drug treatment center after they put me on sedatives was going to my first session with my parents and a psychiatrist my first week there (the first psychiatrist I'd seen in a while). I was taken to his office by the orderlies out of the blue one morning. When I walked into a small office, I saw my parents sitting on a couch. This was the first sighting of my parents since being straitjacketed and drugged. I felt so broken and sad. So humiliated. I just wanted to get on my knees and beg my parents to take me back.

Instead, we got the shit roll for a psychiatrist. He was a total dick. Instantly aggressive and narcissistic. He sat in front of us in his cold office with stone-cold silence. Re-reading my case folder for a minute or two while visually impressing to us that he didn't have time to read our case beforehand. He was obviously a very important man.

I believe that as soon as he read that I had touched drugs and alcohol, his mind was made up. Possibly before that. I saw that look in his eyes. I didn't know it at the time, but I sensed something was off. I could feel something cold behind his veil. I was a cash cow to him. There was no warmth or love here.

He convinced my parents that I needed to continue to be kept on heavy sedation through pills. They said "no." He insisted.

My mom would later confess to me that the psychiatrist had implied after I left that I was suicidal and might commit suicide like her brother had when he was a teen if they took me off of the Ativan. I don't ever remember mentioning or thinking of suicide during my stay. He played my mom while I wasn't there.

During our next session the following week, the psychiatrist was suddenly excited and giddy to tell us about this new Christ-centered long-term drug treatment center. It was only thirty minutes away from Collierville. It was called Second Chance Ministries, Inc. and was sponsored by a local non-denominational Memphis church, Central Church.

The psychiatrist had a Second Chance brochure that he gave us. His biggest push to my parents was that there was a 95% success rate and that I'd be out in three to six months max. In return, they would get a respectable Christian young adult who contributed to the family and society, free from the yoke and bondage of substance abuse.

His biggest push to me was that all of the other kids and staff at Second Chance were amazing, he'd personally been there and would continue to see me, and I'd get to ride horses on daily field trips (seriously) with the other kids.

He then assured my parents that the homeschooling choices were also elite at Second Chance and provided by a local private Christian school. They were sold. Just an up-front payment of $10,000 to Second Chance Ministries, Inc., since it wasn't covered by anyone's health insurance (he said they had a payment plan if my parents needed it).

"But trust me," said the psychiatrist, "Second Chance is backed by the Memphis mega church, Central Church. You have certainly heard of Central Church, haven't you?"

Almost everyone in the surrounding 50-mile radius of Memphis had heard of Central Church at that time. My parents certainly had. He then made sure to mention to my parents, again, the "95%" success rate and that I'd be out in three to six months. Hook, line, and sinker.

Since I hadn't done anything "wrong" other than run away from home, and there was no official medical diagnosis that would support insurance paying for me to go to a long-term drug treatment center; my parents' health insurance was only willing to pay for thirty days of short-term treatment and then outpatient therapy.

So, my parents had a quandary on their hands. It was either take me back in a couple of weeks and go through outpatient family drug and alcohol therapy with their fifteen-year-old son, which previously failed multiple times with their other son, or spend $10,000. They took a gamble and spent $10,000.

I would later find out that the $10,000 my parents paid to reserve my spot at Second Chance that day was non-refundable as soon as they signed the papers. At any point, as soon as they gave their signature on the papers, $10,000 was gone. Poof.

However, they were sure they could trust Central Church, even though it was non-denominational, right? I was literally, unknowingly to my parents, sold off that day.

The next few weeks didn't matter much at the treatment center after that. I was designated for Second Chance. The one thing I positively remember, other than a gloriously layered chocolate cake in their cafeteria during lunch, is that I finally got to go outside once during that stay to play on the short-term treatment center's rope course; a course set-up on their property in the trees led by trained staff. It was fun. I only got to do it once. It would be the last time I would remember having fun in the woods for a while.

I also remember it being one of the last times I'd be truly myself and silly for a long, long while. I'm a silly person at heart. I love to laugh. There have been many times I have been shamed for my silly actions while in public. I'm sorry.

My first memory of this was in first grade while my class was walking down the hallway. I was positioned toward the back of the line and decided to start half-hopping like a bunny, still keeping pretty much in line and on pace with everyone else. Well, my teacher who was at the front of the line decided to hide around the corner and pop-out as soon as the back of the line was coming around. There I was, hopping like a bunny. She scolded me in front of everyone and instantly sapped my joy away. We were in school, I guess that was not the place to be happy or silly. Silly me.

Another time I remember someone in authority scolding me for being silly was during those last few weeks at the short-term drug treatment center. It mirrored my first experience. One day some of the other kids at the center and I were walking down the hallway and being led into a room for a group rap by one of the orderlies. I was lingering in the back of the group of kids and had, for some unfathomable reason, started hopping like a bunny towards the room's entry.

I don't know, maybe it was the hospital gown I had on, or the fact that I had been on a heavy dose of benzodiazepines, but for some reason I was happy at the time and decided to hop. The orderly did not like that. He turned around and scolded me just like my second-grade teacher, further stuffing my fun and silly side deep inside of me. I straightened up and walked as they wanted me to walk. Not cool man, not cool.

Part 2

Captivity

Chapter 9
Ride to Second Chance
(Should've been run away attempt #3)
November 1991

Several weeks later, my health insurance was up at the short-term center, and I'm taking a ride to Second Chance with my parents in their car. I didn't really make any real strides while at the short-term center and never shared my secret there. I still don't understand how something like that exists and how that form of a system could be allowed to treat our children. I hope things have changed. However, I've heard through the grapevine that our treatment centers for adolescents haven't changed much over the years.

The ride to Second Chance with my parents in the backseat of their car was a quiet and somber one. I was still heavily stoned on pills that had been part of my steadily prescribed diet the past few weeks, pills I couldn't even get on the "street," and completely stunned about what was going on. I couldn't really process it at all at the time. It was too much.

I had one chance to escape when my dad decided to stop at the gas station on the way there. I was left in the car with my mom, her in the front seat, me in the back. I remember slowly thinking about running; I seriously considered it. However, I was sedated and remembered thinking "I get to ride horses. It can't be that bad, I'll be back in school and with my friends in no time."

I should've run.

Chapter 10
Second Chance intake

After the brief stop, my parents and I rolled into an industrial section of Memphis, Tennessee. Memphis is a huge distribution center city with a lot of warehouse districts. Second Chance was in one of those districts, and inside one of those abandoned warehouse spaces.

We turned into a huge industrial complex of one-story concrete warehouses, around ten large buildings in all, and took a long drive to one of the buildings in the back. Seeing the sign on the door of one of the tenant spaces in the back warehouse: Second Chance Ministries, Inc., my parents parked, and I grudgingly followed them through another large and mainly vacant parking lot and then through the front door of my new prison.

It was a tiny reception area, filled with a receptionist sitting at a desk across from a small couch. We checked in and waited on the tiny couch. I'm pretty sure that I had to awkwardly stand so my parents could sit down.

About ten minutes later, a lady, who looked to be in her mid-forties and had the disposition of an evil witch, appeared. She was accompanied by a teenaged boy who looked a little older than me and had a very serious look on his face, almost like he was mean mugging me. He was an obviously older and stouter, but shorter, dude. I remember thinking, "dude, why are you staring me down?" and "lady, why are you so cold?" As if she heard my thoughts, she demanded in a cold and calculating voice for me to please follow them.

We traveled down a hallway, took a right turn through a doorway, and entered a small room. She sat down at the desk. There were two chairs in front of the desk. I sat down in one and the teenaged boy sat down in the other.

She introduced herself and then proceeded to explain to me that I was at a Christian long-term drug treatment center for adolescents. I proceeded to look at her with a doped look on my face, because I was seriously doped at the time; an expression of "what the hell are you talking about?" She then began to lay it out for me in significantly terrifying detail.

She explained that Second Chance was a non-profit (yea, right) daytime treatment center of approximately fifty kids, a few junior and senior staff, a few executive staff, and a couple of graduates who were still on their Aftercare. The drug treatment center had taken the twelve-step philosophy of Alcoholics Anonymous and, instead of using "Higher Power," they had inserted "Christ" into the twelve-step program instead. Their entire model of treatment was built this way.

She then bluntly informed me that I would learn how to be a good Christian teenager for my parents. She handed me several paper packets from across the desk and told me to carefully pay attention.

The first packet we went over was an explanation of Second Chance's phases of recovery. There were five phases plus an Aftercare phase.

Being that I'm a "first phaser," I would be attending this center during the day and then taken to another programmer's parents' house who lived in-town in the late afternoon. There, I would eat dinner and stay the night with the foster family, and they would return me to the center in the morning. I was considered a "newcomer." The family would be my "host family" for the night. The other programmer would be considered my "oldcomer."

Until I had earned advancement, I would be led around by the "hand of friendship," always given by an oldcomer, unless I was sitting down. It didn't matter if I was at the center or at the host home.

The first advancement in phase one was called "Talk." This meant that I could have the privilege of talking to my parents for ten minutes with an oldcomer present after Friday night group raps.

The second and last advancement on first phase was "Talk and Responsibility (T&R)," which meant that I could be trusted off the "hand of friendship." Instead, an oldcomer would walk beside me holding onto my shirt. I had no idea what she was talking about when she said, "hand of friendship." It sounded nice though.

After the first phase came the second phase, when I would become an oldcomer. Since my parents lived in town, I was going to be able to go home at night with them when I reached that phase. I would still attend the center during the day. We would be required to become a foster family and host the out-of-town teens and other newcomers at the drug treatment center during the remainder of my treatment.

The third phase, which I would quickly find out wasn't even halfway through their progression timewise, allowed me to attend a local high school that supported the Second Chance program, Germantown High. I would have strict rules, as you will see, but I would accompany other kids in the program to public school. My high school used to play Germantown High in sports all the time, so I was already vaguely familiar with the school.

Fourth phase advancement meant I would be able to have additional privileges like watching PG-rated television and movies and also listening to approved Christian-only music. In addition, I was allowed to go on an outing with my parents once a week.

Fifth phase, I could go to church with my parents on Sunday instead of going to the center's service. I could also go to two outings a week with my parents where I could invite other 5th phasers to join us.

Fifth phase was the last phase before graduation of the treatment program. 5th phasers were asked to stand by the side of group while not in school and grant minor requests to the other programmers of their gender, such as emergency bathroom visits.

After graduation, I would be required to complete an additional six months of intensive Second Chance Aftercare.

She then calmly explained that each phase typically took three to six months to complete, and that there were frequent setbacks. Anyone, at any time, could be demoted back phases if the Second Chance senior or executive staff deemed it necessary.

So, she explained, if one of us "programmers" breaks a minor rule, we could be demoted back one phase and made to repeat that phase over. If we broke a major rule, like relapse somehow, Second Chance could make us restart the entire treatment, even if we were in Aftercare.

I did some quick math and said, "that means I won't be off Aftercare until almost two years from now." She grinned and said "correct."

I then said, "I thought this was going to only last six months max." She coldly replied that, "though possible to complete the treatment phases in six months, no one had been able to do it in under a year so far. The typical completion time is eighteen months to two years for someone around your age."

I was stunned silent.

She then took that opportunity to review the second packet she had given me. It was a long list of all the rules. It was a thick packet.

The first, and most important, rule was Honesty. I was required to be honest at all times at the center and anytime I was not at the center.

The rest of the major "no-no's" in the paper packet included: no drugs (even over-the-counter or prescription) unless approved by staff first; no alcohol (not even in baked goods); no caffeine; no tobacco use of any kind; absolutely no talking at the center unless directed to do so by staff; no talking behind backs; no reading unless approved to do so and it's an approved material; no watching of television, radio, or other forms of media; no singing unless in group led exercises; no talking back to oldcomers; no talking on the phone; no dating or any type of physical relationship with anyone; no communication of any kind to anyone outside of the center; no fraternizing with pairs of opposite sexes (always had to have an odd number, the only exception being our parents); and no "druggie language" (couldn't say a long list of words, including: cool, dude, radical, awesome, far out, groovy, man, weird, damn, and any other word that came anywhere close to being associated to a curse word, the druggie culture, or hippie lifestyle).

I was stunned again. Two years, with these rules!?!

I exclaimed "Where the hell are the horses, don't we go horseback riding?" She just lightly laughed. A twinkle forming in her eye, a spark of life in her mad soul, and said, "I don't know where you could have heard such a ridiculous lie." My heart sank at that moment. I'm not sure it's ever recovered.

She then said, "we will now lead you back to the rap group that is in session. You are not allowed to talk to anyone in group without permission, to stay seated, and to pay attention at all times."

What happened next, I still can't believe I allowed. She nodded to the teenage boy sitting next to me and, while standing up from his chair, he announced to me that he would now show me the "hand of friendship."

He then, while standing behind me, pushed me forward in my chair with his left hand on my left shoulder. He reached down and put his right hand into the back of my pants and placed his thumb through the back belt loop while grabbing my pants tightly in a fist. At the same time, he said loudly "this is the 'hand of friendship,' I know you are having a hard time trusting yourself at this time so I will do it for you." He then lifted me up out of the seat, gave me a huge wedgie, and forced me to walk forward on my tippy toes.

I guess I didn't fight back because I was in shock and sedated at the time. I don't know, I really wish I had at least tried, but at the same time I'm glad I didn't hurt anyone. I knew by that time that seriously hurting someone physically was something I could never take back.

He forcibly walked me out the door on the "hand of friendship" as we followed the senior staff person. We marched down the short corridor, through a doorway, and proceeded into a very large room that was a converted warehouse receiving room with two closed garage bay doors at the end. This would become the main space that I would spend the majority of my next two years in.

It was a large space that was divided into three rooms. Two of the rooms were small rooms in the rear, one for a lunchroom and the other for small group rap therapy. The third and much larger room with the docking bays was in the front and accessed through the small group rap room.

In the middle of the third room were ten rows of old church pews, four pews in each row. The pews were evenly separated by a large center aisle way. This was the main group area and where we would see our parents on Friday night (more on that in a moment). The whole space had a commercial acoustic tile ceiling grid system throughout that consisted of bright 1980s fluorescent tube lights and dingy white ceiling tiles chocked full of holes.

I walked on the front balls of my feet, so as not to give myself a wedgie, into the small group therapy room. Sitting in the room was a group of about fifteen teens, varying in ages, arranged in a large circle on the floor doing crafts. They were separated by sex, with boys on one side of the circle and girls on the other. The dude gripping me tightly in the "hand of friendship" then forcibly sat me down on my butt on the boys' side of the circle and said, quietly in my ear, "you can make some Christmas crafts with the rest of the group if you want."

Sitting in a pile on the floor in front of me were small stacks of differently colored sheets of construction paper, child-proof scissors, tape, Elmer's glue, and crayons. I curiously looked around the room and saw everyone intently staring down at their own paper snowmen, Christmas trees, and snowflakes that they were making. In a highchair, sitting at the head of the circle, was another staff member who also looked to be in her mid-forties. She was mainly paying attention to and making notes in a large notebook binder she held in her lap.

Nobody would make eye contact with me. There was absolute silence, no smiles or acknowledgement. To top it all off, the teens were in plain church clothes with no ties or belts. It was so sad. It was also extremely scary. Almost "Children of the Corn" scary.

I eventually tried to stare down the boy sitting to the right of me. He looked up. I nodded, smiled, and said "hey." He quickly looked back down. I then heard the staff person who was sitting in the highchair sternly warn me that there was to be no talking and to focus on my crafts. Ok, fuck.

I just sat there in a daze. As I glanced around the room, I saw all of the twelve steps that I already knew oh so well emblazoned in placards on the walls. One placard for each step. Only, now, the words "Higher Power" were replaced with "Jesus Christ" and there was a corresponding scripture verse below each step. I would soon have those placards and verses well memorized.

Ok, fuck. I was so screwed. I loved the idea of Jesus Christ and everything, but this was too much. I remember thinking that I had all of a sudden entered the Temple of Jerusalem where the Bible says that Christ overturned all of the money changing tables and announced it as a Den of Thieves. I didn't feel like I was in a holy place. If the Holy Spirit was there, It was there to remind us to be strong in the face of desolation. Hope is a real thing. I'm glad I hung on to it.

Chapter 11
First phase (prior to Talk)

Shortly after my rude introduction to Second Chance, the staff member leading the group asked, "who wants to put away the art supplies while we head into the lunchroom?" The darnedest thing then happened. At that moment, every kid in the room started flapping their arms straight out in front of them as hard as they could. I later found out it was called getting "motivated." Some of the kids were definitely getting more "motivated" than others.

The staff member then called on one of the more ambitious arm flappers, and they got up and started putting away the crafts. I went to rise with the rest of the group and quickly found a hand on my shoulder forcing me back down. Oh ya, I forgot, the "hand of friendship."

It was my friend from intake just a few moments earlier. He even said the "hand of friendship, having a hard time trusting yourself" mantra again as his hand snaked inside my back waistline. He said it in my ear. We all said it in each other's ears when it was our turn to be oldcomers.

As I would come to find out, there was joy in pulling a newcomer up by their pants as hard as one could. First, we got away with it. Second, as was wanting to happen a lot due to frequent demotions at Second Chance, we sometimes ended up becoming the oldcomer to someone who used to be our oldcomer and gave us wedgies not so long ago. Sweet, sweet revenge.

It was creepy to say the least, but I let this guy lead me by the back of my pants to the small lunchroom and be placed down at a metal folding chair at a folding table. There were two rows of folding tables separated by about six feet. One row was for the boys, the other side for the girls. It was dead quiet.

On a center folding table at the front of the room sat a couple of buffet style chafing pans with lit warming candles. I was served by one of the two oldcomers that had gone earlier to set up before I had arrived at the lovely craft-fest group. It was some of the foulest cafeteria food I'd ever seen or eaten. Dry, cold, skin-on chicken breast with a side of mashed potatoes, and a cubed vegetable medley.

I picked at it with my fork and bravely tried to take a bite. It was utterly disgusting; I couldn't eat it. I found out in my later phases that it was leftover food donated from Central Church. Leftovers from the previous day's church luncheons for their elderly. Instead of tossing it out, Central Church would happily donate it to us. After all, we were non-profit, so I'm sure it was a tax write off. I would soon learn to eat it no matter how many days I knew it had been sitting in the lunchroom refrigerator. The oldcomers were allowed to bring sack lunches from home. Hunger strikes from newcomers were frequent.

So, after everyone except myself vigorously ate their food, I was put on the "hand of friendship" with the other newcomers of the group and led into the large main room. In the middle of the room were ten to twelve rows of old church pews with a large aisle separating the boy pews from the girl pews. This never changed. We were never allowed on the other side of the pews. It didn't matter who we were, it was never ok, unless we were executive staff. I never saw anyone brazen enough to try.

I was parked by the oldcomer carrying me on the "hand of friendship" into a spot in the second row from the front, not the first row. I surmised at the time that this was strategic. I would later learn I was right. Second Chance staff liked to put all "flight risks" in the second pew and have oldcomers sit on the sides of the third and first pews; ready to tackle the newcomers if they decided to make a run for it.

No one was able to freely escape the center without getting tackled by most of the older teens surrounding them. The oldcomers were strongly encouraged by staff to tackle and restrain anyone. I guess that since it was kids tackling other kids it didn't count as abuse?

These teens were desperate to tackle any kid and get rewarded. Hell, I did the tackling just for the kick of it when it was my turn to be an oldcomer. I felt like a defensive corner in football, just daring the other team to throw the ball into my zone.

So, I got sandwiched into the second-row pew, and two staff members (one senior and one junior) sat in highchairs in front of the pews. After everyone sat down, I heard one of the staff members say, "Brian, can you please stand up and introduce yourself to the group?" So, I stood, and being as honest as I could, introduced myself and said, "I think I'm in the wrong place, I don't really understand how I ended up here." I then listed my meager drug use and experiences.

Now, as soon as I uttered those words, the other kids in the pews, a few at first, started flapping their arms (getting motivated). Then, the entire group was arm flapping. It looked and sounded like a flock of geese taking flight, it was fucking ridiculous. I even started laughing while I was talking, I could not help it.

About ten seconds in of fierce motivating on behalf of the group, and me standing there thinking: "oh man, this can't be real, these kids look mad," one of the staff leading the group rap called on one of the more motivated arm flappers. They stood, and I got "challenged" in group for the first time.

Now, what getting challenged in group meant in Second Chance was that we were in big time trouble because we broke the most important rule: Honesty. Another "programmer" (someone who was also a patient in the drug treatment center) would chide you in front of the whole group and talk crap about you, list all your faults, and venomously spew to everyone that what you did was extremely un-Christlike (like they would fucking know). The verbal abuse was meant to be humiliating and demeaning, while still following all the program's rules.

The staff who were leading the group, and any straggling staffers that happened to be in the back watching, were then alerted by the vocal challenge. Whatever you got challenged about would be recorded in their logbooks, and, if you got enough challenges from the group, you had to go back a phase. Not what you wanted to have happen.

However, for me, it didn't really matter. I was a newcomer doing what I would eventually find out was called "sitting" at the rehabilitation center. "Sitting" meant I was moping about in my head and not "working" the "program." I was "sitting" in my "recovery." Sitting was routine for all new programmers, or those that had been demoted back to the first phase.

So, this teen stood and began to vehemently scold me in front of the group for at least two minutes, saying "I don't believe you or your short drug list. It is obvious that you are lying to us. You need to get in touch with your real feelings and start praying that Jesus will open up your heart to your truth. You need to practice the first step, admit you are powerless to drugs and alcohol, and only then can Jesus save you. Until you admit the truth, we will continue to challenge you."

I just stood there in a stupor while all of these other kids stared at me. That kid sat down, and the other kids started motivating again. I sat the fuck down. Staff called on at least three other kids to chide me while I sat there on that church pew with my head in the palms of my hands. It was brutal.

After the verbal chiding, one of the staff finally said, "that's enough" and followed it with, "Brian, believe it or not, we were both newcomers just like you, over four years ago, and in the exact same situation you will continue to be in until you admit you have a drug and alcohol problem and turn to Jesus for forgiveness."

I wasn't laughing anymore. I just sat there for the rest of the afternoon. I continued "sitting" for a while. It would be a while longer still until I could truly laugh again.

Group rap continued for the rest of the afternoon with various challenges thrown among the "programmers" to other "programmers" and tons of sad stories of past drug and alcohol abuse that were obviously way overly romanticized in a negative way to illicit feelings and be able to share those feelings (i.e., tears) with the group. There were lots of feelings and blame shared. I just sat there in a daze, feeling extremely nauseous.

I was smart enough at that time to realize what was happening at this "program," and the shit was adding up in my tiny mind as I sat there in a daze. Oh, fuck. Every kid in here, including myself, was truly fucked.

Towards the end of the rap, the rest of the oldcomers started trickling in by small groups from the various schools they had been shuttled to and from that day. One group at a time. By the end, we had a large group of about forty to fifty teenaged kids and started a quick afterschool rap session.

After hearing various challenges by the "oldcomers" to other "oldcomers" where they had seen a minor rule broken, more fake stories about their negative past drug use situations to the group, more fake tears (most were so obviously fake), more arm flapping, and more blame; we concluded afterschool rap.

We sat quietly in the pews while the 5thphasers peeled off to the back of the room and started collecting and distributing suitcases and backpacks to the other programmers. More staff started rolling in, about five in total now, and they conferred over a clipboard for around twenty minutes. Us kids continued to sit in silence, with the occasional quiet reminder from a 5th phaser, standing on the side of the pews, that we needed to "get out of our heads" and not think "negative thoughts."

How one can sit in silence and not "get in their head" nor "think negative thoughts" while being told not to do so at the same time puzzled the hell out of me. How was that possible? That was some crazy talk right there.

A staff member then started naming host family assignments; directing us programmers to the home we were going to, or the host mates we would have at our home. Always of the same naturally assigned sex. As if that mattered. I was a large kid and luckily none of the host homes I stayed at tried to sexually or physically abuse me. I've heard that some of the other kids that went through Second Chance weren't so lucky.

We never really knew whose home we were going to until that day's assignments. Even if we usually went to our own home and were on one of the higher phases, we could be summoned to another oldcomer's host home to assist if needed.

The oldcomer's parents didn't know either. They would patiently sit in their cars in the parking lot each night until staff came out and shouted the nightly assignments through cracked car windows.

Eventually my name was called, and I was assigned to a host family for the night. Then, shortly after, I was picked up by the "hand of friendship" by an oldcomer. He was now to become my oldcomer for the night. An additional oldcomer was assigned with him for support, or to help restrain me if I tried to run.

Out the side door, down a set of wooden stairs, into the parking lot, with my suitcase and backpack in tow, I went. Being wedgied the entire way by the "hand of friendship." Into the backseat of his parents' car I was placed, and off to his parents' house, with his dad driving, we paraded away. All of the programmers spreading out across the Memphis metropolitan area and traveling to our respective destinations for the night.

In our particular car, the three of us programmers sat in the backseat with my tall 6'3" ass crammed into the middle. Everyone in the car introduced themselves to me. They seemed nice. My oldcomer said I could then talk if I wanted and announced that their house was forty minutes away.

Sitting there in the middle of the car backseat on that long ride to God knows where, squished into the shape of a ball by my confines, was the first time I ever heard the ever-nefarious phrase "Brian, what are you thinking about?" used in such an insidious and spiteful way. It was being directed to me by my oldcomer.

Now, I never knew until that moment that anyone could turn such a polite phrase into such an evil question. I still get triggered to this day when I hear those words from others, even loved ones. I must pause in that moment and remind myself that it was probably meant and said in a caring way, even though I feel consumed by rage most of the time when I hear it. Why we said it in treatment was not because we cared.

I just sat there, quietly staring in front of me out the car's front windshield, while my oldcomer kept rudely and loudly repeating to me "Brian, what are you thinking about?" After thirty or so seconds, I couldn't take it, and I made the classic newcomer mistake of saying "nothing." His eyes lit up and, taking in a deep breath before he railed on me, he proceeded to challenge me in his most authoritative voice on how I had just broken the number one rule, Honesty, because I couldn't have been thinking of "nothing." He was going to challenge me in the morning in group for lying to him.

He then said, "Brian, you were sitting in your head, thinking negative thoughts, and until you confess to those thoughts, you will continue to sit." He queried aloud whether I was thinking about running and told me that if I did, he and the other oldcomer would happily restrain me. The other oldcomer piped in that he eagerly supported that idea as well. I would find out later on when I was an oldcomer that this was standard tradition passed down from one oldcomer to another. Unfortunately, the emotional hazing never stopped at Second Chance.

We arrived around six o'clock that evening, and my oldcomer's dad parked the car in the carport. It was very dark by then, and I could feel their nervousness in the air while they were outside with me. I wasn't going to run, didn't even consider it to be honest. I really wanted to see how this all played out. There was an odd part of me that thought maybe this was all a test and that I'd be riding unicorns that shat rainbows the next day. Hey, one can dream. Don't shame.

So, in his driveway in the pitch-black dark, my oldcomer reached down into the backseat (risking being elbowed in the nose by me) and grabbed the back of my pants by the "hand of friendship." Somehow, he was able to haul me by my back center belt loop all the way out of the car and to his parents' front door. I would learn how to do that trick later. The other oldcomer stood by, daring me to try and run.

Through the front door, down a hallway, and into a kitchen I was led by the backseat of my pants. My newcomer parked me in a chair at the kitchen dinner table. He and the other newcomer sat beside me.

While dinner was being prepared, I was handed a few sheets of notebook paper and a pencil by my oldcomer. He calmly explained that every night during dinner preparation, I was to write what was called a Moral Inventory (or MI report for short). He then drew out several squares of different sizes on one piece of paper and, placing the sheet of paper in front of me, showed me where to write my name, date, current phase, and number sequence in the upper right square.

The second large square on the sheet was for me to write down a negative drug story I had before I came here. I was then to scribe how I felt about that memory in my third square.

I sat at the kitchen table in a completely fugue state, still in shock by what all had occurred that day, and nothing came to mind. I wrote my name in the upper right-hand corner; I could remember that. I drew a blank on everything else. My first MI report was blank, except for some lines to delineate squares, my name, 1st phase, and a "#1" in the upper right-hand corner.

We ate a simple solemn meal that the oldcomer's parents fixed for us, and, after supper, I was led by the "hand of friendship" into the living room. While parking my butt on the couch, my oldcomer explained to me that this was the time when we were supposed to discuss our new MI report entries with the rest of the host family. Sometimes the siblings would join us in the living room and listen in if they were old enough. A lot of times those very same siblings would end up in Second Chance themselves as programmers. Keep it in the family, I guess.

Since I was a newcomer, I was required to write each day about one negative time in my druggy past when I used alcohol and/or drugs, and how I felt about it. To this day it makes me extremely happy to think about because I have a fond memory of when someone at Second Chance once courageously wrote "Fuck you" in all of the squares on their first MI report. They got challenged in group several times because of it. They eventually had to take a Sharpie to it, cross out the fucks, and write-in the word "Love" above them in order to advance in the program. "Love you," "Fuck you"; such endearing terms of expression.

I would find out the next day that we were to bring our MI report logbook binders into the center with us every morning. We were supposed to stack the binders at the back of the room when we arrived at the rehabilitation center each morning, our names labeled for staff. Staff would then peruse those MI reports during the day to keep check on everyone and challenge us in group if needed.

After MI report sharing, my oldcomer led me by the "hand of friendship" into the hallway bathroom. He stood inside the bathroom with me, guarding the door, while I did my business, all the while verbally challenging me about being in my head. He then led me from the hall bathroom to his bedroom on "the hand of friendship." I was kept in the bedroom under supervision while each oldcomer left to separately attend to their own bathroom needs.

I first learned about magnetic door and window alarms and pee jugs when my oldcomers were done.

First, the door and window alarms. Every host family's oldcomer's bedroom, no matter the phase they were on, had cheap magnetic alarms on both the door and windows that were turned on and off by a key. The windows could open, but they would make a god-annoying sound and wake everyone up. The door could also open, but it too would sound. There was no good way of sneaking out unnoticed. The parents didn't have to worry about locking anything.

Second, the pee jug. While laughing, my two oldcomer pals introduced me to the pee jug and explained this is where I should go to relieve myself in the middle of the night. It was a milk jug with an opening cut out of the top. My oldcomer said, "Don't spill it."

My nights from there on out for the next eighteen months were filled with waking up several times each night to the sound and smell of someone peeing in a pee jug. I don't know what the girls did to be honest. I want to say they had a pee bucket with a lid, but I'm not sure.

I was then told by my oldcomers that they would be extremely mad if I needed to go poo and wake everyone up just so a parent could unlock the door alarm. Point taken.

What I remember most about that night was lying on the floor in a sleeping bag and listening to these kids talk to one another in what I could best describe as a new language. They were chatting on and on about listening to Christian music, discussing Bible verses, and how much they loved Jesus. They didn't talk shit about anyone or to each other, at all. In fact, they weren't allowed to talk about or name anyone else outside of the bedroom, not even their parents or siblings, unless they were very popular in approved Christian culture (the president, Christian artists, Bible figures, etc.).

They were still creative in how they said things too. It wasn't like they were dumb, and I couldn't follow along because of that, but the way they organized sentences to avoid pronouns or talking behind backs was completely foreign to me. You couldn't even use a pronoun of anyone when telling a story unless they were there in the room. It is very difficult to convey a message verbally that way without lots of practice. Let alone tell a story.

These kids were doing just that and not making mistakes either. It was like they were trying to one-up each other. Secretly scared the other one might challenge them in group the next day.

So, me being the typical dumbass I am, asked out loud "do y'all think the Grateful Dead could be considered Christian music? I really like them." I halfway meant it too.

Being a fan, I had read that the Grateful Dead were based on the Christian motif story of the Grateful Dead found in the Dead Sea Scrolls Book of Tobit. The band felt at the time that this best portrayed how they felt in front of a live audience; grateful that the audience appreciated their music, and in turn, they would continue producing the best live music they could for the audience.

I also knew there was nothing evil about the group and its lyrics. Quite the opposite in my opinion. The Grateful Dead constantly sung about love and had numerous Christian references in their songs, and, since I knew lots of Christians that listened to them, were they not a Christian group?

Ya, me naming that band didn't go over well with them. The oldcomers did not want to hear any of that, they were certain I was wrong. I barely got ten words in, and I was challenged for the next five minutes on how I should never mention that evil band again and that they were Satan's music. My bad, how dare I?

As I was curling up in the sleeping bag on the floor, fuming silently over this, my oldcomer said from his bed, in a sincere tone, "Brian, what are you thinking about?" After I didn't answer him a few times, he then went on a one-minute spill challenging me to get out of my head. It silently dawned on me, "My God, this never stops."

I didn't sleep much that night. I tried to sing Grateful Dead songs in my head, but I couldn't come up with the lyrics. I was too scared. I was too scared to even count sheep.

Next morning, way before the butt-crack of dawn, I was woken up to both oldcomers serenading me loudly with merrily glee: "rise and shine, and give God your glory, glory; rise and shine, let's wake up and go to drug treatment." Then they repeated it several times, loudly, yelling the song at me.

It became a song I would hear repeatedly yelled at other newcomers and oldcomers every morning for the next eighteen months. It even got to the point where I felt obligated to sing it to my newcomers. I still wake up sometimes with that tune stuck in my head. I'm usually silently screaming the song at myself.

After the horrible rise and shine, my oldcomer carried me by belt loop to the bathroom where we took turns showering, got dressed, and ate a quick breakfast that the host parents had prepared (ranging from oatmeal to snack bars to fruit). This always depended on the host family – some host families were poor and could only afford very meager food, and a few of the rich host parents would have a breakfast buffet splayed out in front of us in their kitchen by their chef. That morning's choice was cereal. I love cereal.

My oldcomer's parents, while it was still dark, drove us back to the rehabilitation center for our morning therapy. Our suitcases and backpacks in tow.

Once back inside Second Chance, my oldcomer led me into the large room with pews. We sat our stuff down, and my oldcomer parked my butt on a pew with the rest of the group and sat next to me. The room was deafeningly silent. Just slight shuffling. Talking in group without permission was not allowed.

Suddenly, my oldcomer started getting motivated and flapped his arms wildly in front of him. About eight to ten seconds into his motivation, a staff member from up front called his name. He then stood and proceeded to challenge me in front of the group. The staff member asked me to stand; I rudely refused. My oldcomer then said directly to me, him standing up, me sitting down, that he was disappointed that I was "sitting" and "in my head" all last night. He let me know that I "wouldn't get anywhere sitting," and then he challenged me to talk about it in morning group rap (when he conveniently wouldn't be there).

He then sat down and raised his hand half-way up to signal to a 5th phaser standing on the side that he was ready to be excused to go to school. I was like, "Dude, what the hell?"

Chapter 12
The Cassidys (Scotty and Jean)

After my very rude oldcomer left for school, all of the other oldcomers above the second phase proceeded to leave in small groups to go to one of the three assigned high schools, leaving the 1st and 2nd phasers in the pews. After everyone left for school, we started our morning group rap.

As soon as the rap got underway, I was immediately stood by staff and questioned why I looked so down? I refused to stand or say anything. They laughed, as did some others in the group, and went on with the rap, asking the group to share their negative drug use stories and feelings (which basically meant to try to cry without getting caught embellishing).

The morning raps continued on in that fashion until shortly before lunchtime, when, in the middle of a rap, the programmer sharing in group stopped talking, everything got dead quiet, and I turned around to look where everyone else was looking. Walking up to the pews was a middle-aged, Scottish American lady, probably in her mid-fifties. There seemed to be a gloom surrounding her. She did not look like a pleasant person to me. Instead, she looked more like "The Church Lady" character on Saturday Night Live with a Scottish Southern American upbringing.

She walked through the center aisle and proudly waltzed up to the middle of the group. She didn't even pause to say excuse me to the group, or the girl standing and sharing at the time. Standing near my pew, she said, in a very loud, authoritative, and thickly accented voice, "Brian Quattlebaum! Please stand up." Almost as if verbally compelled, I stood.

She introduced herself to me as Mrs. Jean Cassidy, the Reverend's wife, and explained that her and the Reverend ran the place together. She then, in a very serious and scolding Scottish tone with a Southern American twang, continued to chide me for several minutes, challenging me why I was just "sitting," "in my head," and "stuck in my negative thoughts."

She wouldn't let me talk. She just kept talking. Towards the end she said, "Brian, I know you're a smart young man. I think you'll figure out this program in no time." Then she fucking winked at me. It was one of those winks a hunter gives its prey after it traps it. I just sat right back down. The rap continued.

After the morning raps, and a brief ten-minute exercise where we stood outside of the pews and shook out our muscles by flapping our limbs everywhere, hilariously accidentally hitting everyone beside us, we went into the lunchroom; me being wedgied the whole way by the "hand of friendship."

Served to us was the same leftover refrigerated lunch from yesterday: at least four-day-old broiled chicken with some of the skin still on it and a vegetable medley that had no recognizable vegetables in it. The vegetable melody consisted of cubes of several colors that had zero taste. It didn't matter the color. Oh, and some of the driest mashed potatoes I'd ever had. I would have rather bitten into a raw potato. At least I would have gotten a bit of moisture out of the bite. I continued to decline eating it.

After lunch, we had more group raps. During one of them, a smaller man, possibly in his late fifties, came in and, interrupting the rap in a Scottish voice with a hint of a Southern twang, asked for me. When an oldcomer went to get me, he said "no, no, it's ok, Brian doesn't need the hand of friendship or an oldcomer right now." I thought, "Shit, hallelujah!" I was certain that somehow my parents had a change of heart and had come to rescue me. I was elated.

I strolled down that corridor like a peacock, proudly marching like a free man right behind the Reverend. We went past the lobby and waltzed into a giant room up front, his office. It was vacant. He shut the door and asked me to take a seat.

I placidly sat down across from him in his large office with plush furniture and nice air conditioning, between us a really nice wooden desk. On the desk was a large frame of George Bush, Sr.; turned around so that good ole' George was smiling right at me. In the center of the desk was a large name plate that read "Reverend F. Scotty Cassidy."

He introduced himself as the Reverend Scotty Cassidy, Scottish if I didn't know, and that he was the Executive Director of Second Chance. He ran this facility with his wife, Jean, whom I'd previously had the honor of meeting. He'd talked to my parents several times in the past couple of days, and he assured me that they loved me and were constantly thinking of me.

He then looked at me and said, "now, Brian, I know you are thinking about running, but please hear me out first. I want you to understand what will happen, as has happened many times before to those sitting in the same situation you are in right now. If you run, you might make it out the door and past the lobby where I have a staff member and oldcomer waiting to tackle you, and, even if you were somehow able to escape this warehouse complex on foot, you will eventually end up being caught and arrested."

He then quickly followed with, "I can have the Memphis police here in a couple of minutes flat. They are very familiar with us and completely support us. We are on the police's quick response list, and they will scour the area, including your old haunting grounds in Collierville, until they find you. After that, you will be detained in the Shelby County Juvenile Detention Center for a couple of days until you go in front of a judge. On that day, one of my staff will be there with your parents, and they will both ask the court to order you to be retained into Second Chance's custody until you are twenty-one, or earlier if we deem you've completed our program to our satisfaction."

He paused, let that sink in, and then continued. "Now, your parents paid a lot of money out of pocket to get you in here, and there's a good reason for that. We have above a 95% success rate; success meaning full graduation of the program including aftercare. If you try to leave, you will be brought back and must repeat this program all over again. There is no escape other than completing the program to me and my wife's satisfaction. You will understand this in time. I've made a promise to your parents that I will turn you into a fine, outstanding young Christian man that they will be proud of, and I intend to keep that promise."

"See lad," he continues, "I used to live in Florida and was a staff member at a long-term drug-treatment center called 'Straight, Inc.' While working at Straight, I had a brilliant idea and came up with a program that mirrored Straight, but also included Jesus Christ's principals. So, when we moved here, I decided to try running my idea through a local Christian church, Central Church. I asked them to sponsor my idea, an integrated Straight program with Christian principles as a business model. Since its Christian, it's easy to claim non-profit tax-exempt status. Central Church of Memphis heard my pitch and agreed to sponsor us. Thus, our program was born, which has now been successful for over five years. A successful program you will learn to adopt. We don't want our success rate going down, now do we?"

Wow, he completely took the wind out of my sails.

He then said, "Cheer up, Brian, it's not that bad. You're a smart lad. If you behave, you'll get to go home to your own bedroom in a couple of months and enjoy your mom's meals. Plus, you only just turned fifteen, so, if you follow the rules and the program, you can possibly be out in time to go to your senior prom. You'll probably never be able to hang out with any of your old friends, but you'll have new friends through Second Chance. Now that's not so bad, is it?"

He quickly stood , said he was a busy man, and opened the door. The old man wasn't bluffing. There, right outside the door, stood an oldcomer and a staff member. The oldcomer came in and put me on the "hand of friendship." Out the door, down the hall, and back to group I went.

I would later find out that "Reverend" was only an honorary title bestowed upon him by Central Church after his sales pitch to them. I don't think he ever had a real church or congregation. We kids were his congregation. Second Chance was his church.

I'm also pretty certain he didn't have a doctorate in anything. I'm not sure if he had a master's degree either. He was a good salesperson and what would have been called at the time "an excellent small businessman."

I can think of a lot of bad words to call Scotty, but I'll spare the reader. I'll let the reader judge for themselves and use what terminology they think is appropriate. To put the reader's conscience at ease, I'd wager it's been said or thought of before about him by someone, somewhere, sometime.

Later that day, while in group rap (we were almost always holding a group rap) and sitting on either the thinly carpeted concrete floor or an old wooden, non-padded pew, something else eye-opening happened.

I glanced back and saw my psychiatrist from the short-term treatment center. I thought to myself, sarcastically, "hey pal" and waved to him.

He didn't look up or even make eye contact with me or anyone else in the center. He just sat in the back pews while going through the staff logs. He left shortly after. It took me a little while to piece together what was going on, but he would occasionally appear to look at staff logs and sign off on the programmers' therapeutic prescription drugs. He was the primary signatory doctor that Second Chance legally needed.

He never talked to any of the kids at length that I knew of, including me. I would continue to see him show up a few times for the next couple of months. I rarely saw him in group after I progressed. I have no clue what eventually happened to him.

A few days later, two of the kids I knew from the short-term drug treatment center, one boy and one girl, were admitted one right after the other. They had the same wonderful psychiatrist that I had. In hindsight, I believe that my psychiatrist was being paid by Second Chance to recruit gullible parents and their kids into Second Chance. We all fit the mold of rebellious, but not real, law breakers. We were all intelligent kids that had been caught doing stupid things. Our families were also intelligent and caring Christians. Most had at least a little bit of savings. We were what Second Chance was looking for, we were its unfinished product.

I personally believe the psychiatrist was paid not only to be the signatory for the programmers' prescription drugs, but his other role was to recruit kids from the other short-term drug treatment center into Second Chance. Since Second Chance was considered a "non-profit" for some reason (even though the Cassidy's both drove new Cadillacs), the psychiatrist was probably also allowed to deduct a lot of the expenses. All at our expense.

For the rest of the week, I continued to "sit" and stew, not participating in group, but not acting out either. Each grueling night was spent bouncing between oldcomers' houses, each different than the host home I was at the night before. I had absolutely no clue where I was going each night, nor how strict my oldcomer or their parents would be.

Chapter 13
Friday night rap

On my first Friday afternoon at Second Chance, right before dinner, I had my second Reverend F. Scotty Cassidy spotting. His wife, Mrs. Cassidy, was warming up the group by having us sing some Christian group songs. I, not singing, watched intently instead as Scotty came strolling in and jubilantly said to the group that he was ready to make the promotional announcements for the week. He then said my name, "Brian Q.," and looked at me. I stood, and he said, "no advancement; I'm disappointed with you."

That went on like this for every kid in the center for the next twenty minutes. They would stand up when their name was called, and Scotty would announce to the group whether or not they advanced. It was always in order from 1st phasers to 5th phasers. On this particular night, one kid had apparently made it to second phase and was "coming home" to his parents. Another kid had advanced to "graduate" to Aftercare. There were no demotions. Everyone was happy. Apparently, my other two buddies from the short-term drug treatment center and I were the worst kids in the group at that time.

We then proceeded to the lunchroom. It was a very lucky night, even for me. Someone was graduating, so no Central Church leftovers. Instead, a shit load of beef tacos from Taco Bell. We got two tacos each and a small cup of soda from a warm two-liter; I was extremely grateful.

After dinner, we all went back to the large room with pews. However, this time, the large empty area in front was set up with rows of chairs turned facing the pews. The oldcomer who had the privilege of having me on the "hand of friendship" led me to the front with all the other programmers and sat me down on the boys' side of the chairs.

A staff member walked up to the front of our group and exuberantly led us into singing more Christian group songs. The programmers cheerfully got motivated so that we could be called on to name a song out loud. If the staff member agreed, we would sing that song as a group.

During my time at Second Chance, I would end up learning more than fifty different Christian or Christian-appropriate songs to sing as a group. Most were extremely silly. I've intentionally forgotten all but a few, on principle.

Shortly after one of the songs, Scotty came into the room, stood in front of us, and picked up a microphone that was on a long cord. He started testing it as we became silent. He then, while queuing us to get ready, said into the microphone, "loved ones, we're ready for you."

The group then burst into song and the door at the back of the room opened. Slowly all of our parents, younger dependents, and any approved guests came strolling in and sat down in the pews like they would in church. We were the choir, all of us sitting in the chairs up front, welcoming them in and singing, horribly I might add, a Christian group song that staff told us to sing.

After everyone was situated, we stopped singing, and the Reverend Scotty walked over to the front of the pews. He warmed the crowd up with a joke, went into a few housekeeping items, and then nodded to a boy sitting in the front row of chairs.

The boy stood with another microphone and a small group of people in the pews rose as well. Scotty Cassidy handed his microphone over to the small group of people, and they introduced themselves to everyone. It was the oldcomer's family. Mom, dad, older sister, and younger sister. They were apparently veterans at this.

The boy then proceeded to introduce himself, how long he'd been there, what phase he was currently on, his long list of drugs, a brief past drug use story, named one thing he was thankful for his parents about, and one thing he was thankful for the program about.

I called bullshit in my mind at the time. No way that young kid ever did crack cocaine and shot heroin up, all at the same time, and on a daily basis. I couldn't believe anyone was buying it.

The microphone eventually got around to me, and my parents stood. I decided to stand, say my name, and was as honest about my previous drug and alcohol use as I would ever be on that microphone: I had used LSD, mushrooms, mainly by myself in my room, and marijuana and alcohol a few times with friends and once by myself. I didn't really have a lot of negative drug and alcohol experiences to share.

In hindsight, I should have dropped the mic on the floor and then sat down. Instead, I just silently stood there, giving Scotty, who was standing close by, enough time to grab the microphone away from my parents. He quickly told me that I needed to get honest with everyone, including my parents; punctuating that I know that I have used drugs and alcohol more times than what I had shared with everyone. He then reminded me, and everyone there, that I would "continue to sit until you get honest with yourself and admit you have a drug and alcohol problem, not only to everyone here, but to Jesus as well. For, Jesus Christ is the only one that can save you from your addiction."

I quickly plopped down into my cold metal folding chair and don't remember exactly what my parents said after getting the microphone back from Scotty. It was a mixture of that they were disappointed in me for not working the program and that they missed me. Whatever they said, it was brief, and they quickly handed the microphone back to Scotty. The Friday night rap proceeded onward.

After several long, grueling hours, Friday night rap finally ended. Those newcomers who had earned "Talk" or "Talk and Responsibilities" were able to spend a couple of minutes of lone time with their approved guests, their oldcomers right beside them, at the back of the pews. The rest of us went to the front of the pews to sit in silence while we received our home assignments for the night.

That night it was announced that I was going home with the same oldcomer as the night before. A plan then slowly started formulating in my head. I stayed up late that night thinking about it; making sure my oldcomer was asleep first so he wouldn't challenge me or notice I was up to something.

Chapter 14
Run away attempt #3

The following day was Saturday, and, since there was no school, we were allowed to sleep in an hour later. My oldcomer woke me, still nice and early before sunrise, still with the same annoying song that every programmer apparently sung, and we went into the bathroom to take our morning showers.

As he had the morning before, my oldcomer made me take my shower first while he stood outside of the shower guarding the door. Then he jumped into the shower while I was changing.

Well, when I got out of the shower, I decided to quickly put my clothes on while rambling about some nonsense of how I wanted to start working the program. He didn't notice. I saw him put shampoo in his hair through the shower curtain opening. That was my chance.

I booked it out of the bathroom, through the living room, grabbed a fireplace tool along the way for a weapon, and ran out the front door; not stopping to get my shoes. I had jeans, a shirt, and a pair of socks on.

I got to the beginning of the cul-de-sac and turned around. My oldcomer was running out his front door, butt-naked, and barefoot; with only a washcloth to cover his privates.

I kept running. He got about halfway down the street, and seeing he wasn't going to catch up with me, stopped and yelled all sorts of cuss words. I was honestly surprised. I didn't know he had it in him. I could sense that he was very pissed.

I ran for a little while, changing streets several times while dodging through neighborhood yards. Then, checking around to make sure I wasn't followed, I dropped the fireplace tool and quickly got off the road, diving into a nearby deep ditch that ran along the woods behind the suburb.

I didn't have shoes on, only sopping wet socks, but I didn't care. I was free! I walked along the side of the ditch, in the cold dark morning, hidden by the embankment, for a good while along a back row of some houses. I was just trying to gain as much distance as possible. My feet were hurting something awful.

Eventually, when daylight was appearing and I could get a clear view, I poked my head up to survey my surroundings. A few of the suburb's houses' backyards were open to the ditch. I then saw, in a house to my left, a couple of ladies sitting in a kitchen through their glass sliding door. They were just sitting there, peacefully having breakfast and coffee and gabbing away.

I must have been an odd sight. Me, tall, skinny, and covered in mud with no shoes on, walking up to their glass slider in their backyard. I tried my best to look as non-threatening as I could; thinking silently, yet loudly, "I come in peace, please don't shoot me."

When I was about twenty feet away, one of the ladies noticed me, stood from the kitchen table, opened the glass slider, and yelled in her most authoritative, Southern voice, "Can I help you?" I yelled back, as politely as I could, "Sorry to disturb y'all, but I'm in a bit of a predicament. I know this looks and sounds odd, but I just escaped an occult and need to get a hold of my Methodist church in Collierville to see if a counselor can come rescue me. I'm not in trouble with the law, I'm just trying to get away from some very bad people. Could I please come in and call my church?"

I then quickly added, "You can look up the church number in the phone book and call them yourselves; they will know my name immediately." She pondered for a second, turned to her girlfriend who just kind of shrugged, and, God bless her heart, she let me in.

As soon as I got inside, she told me to wait in the kitchen while she looked up the Collierville Methodist Church in the phone book. She called them herself. No answer, of course, but she left a message on the answering machine with my name and her phone number.

She and her friend asked me to sit at the kitchen table while we waited, and (bless their hearts again) asked me if I wanted anything to eat. They had bagels, fruit, and coffee. I happily and graciously obliged.

I then, while gorging myself on breakfast, proceeded into a long, half-concocted, half-truth story about how my stepdad was an occult member and had abducted me the day before to take me to his cult. My mom was out-of-town, and the only people that knew the truth were the counselors at Collierville Methodist Church. The law wouldn't help me, but I believed the church would. The ladies seemed to halfway buy this.

Luckily, about thirty minutes into our very odd and uncomfortable conversation, which continued to twist every second by more and more lies concocted on the fly (entangled lies that were twisting taut enough to snap), the phone rang. It was a receptionist from the church who remembered the Quattlebaum name. I quickly jumped on the phone, reminded her that I had been in Methodist Youth Fellowship for several years, and said that I needed help. I asked her if she could get a hold of Mr. Ed, my beloved church counselor.

She called me back a couple of minutes later and said she could do me even one better. She had spoken to Mr. Ed on the phone, and she was willing to drive out there to get me, forty minutes away, and bring me back to the church. God bless her.

Things got a little easier for the next couple of hours. My story had checked out for the most part and the ladies stopped asking a lot of questions. They did feed me though, again.

An hour later, the Collierville Methodist Church receptionist arrived at the address the ladies had given her and picked me up. I could tell on the car ride home that, although she was uncomfortable with the fact that I had escaped a drug and alcohol rehabilitation center, she was more appalled by my description of the rehabilitation center itself. I think she understood I was living in madness and trying to do the best I could to escape it.

She took me back to the Methodist church in Collierville, and I waited there for Mr. Ed while playing basketball in the gym by myself in my dried, bare feet. I felt sane for the first time in a long while. It wouldn't last.

When Mr. Ed arrived, we hugged in the gym, me sobbing, and he took me to his office. I sat down across from a desk and proceeded to spill what had happened since the last time I saw him.

Barely five minutes into my story with Mr. Ed, my parents entered the office door with a Second Chance senior staff member who happened to live nearby. She had been on my parents' call network list given to them by Second Chance in case this happened and met my parents as soon as they arrived. I turned to look at Mr. Ed, and he said to me, "I'm sorry Brian, but you're a youth and they're your parents. I had to alert them as soon as I heard from the church receptionist. Better than the other choice I had of alerting the police."

I wasn't mad at Mr. Ed, I'm still not. He was doing what he believed the law required at the time and being a good person. He didn't know the madness I had stumbled into. Even if he somehow did, he couldn't rescue me.

The senior staff member that came with my parents mainly spoke. She said, "Brian, I've been in your situation, but trust me, this will end in a very bad way if you don't come with us back to the center. Your parents have given me permission to call the Collierville police, and have you arrested for escaping from the center if you don't return to treatment. You will be arrested, and we will have you court-ordered into our care until you are twenty-one."

I looked over at my parents and they both solemnly nodded, my mom sobbing into her hands. I thought to myself, "I'll be damned, that old codger Scotty wasn't bluffing. What a fucking loophole."

My mom would later remiss that the staff member had told them before they entered that they shouldn't listen to anything I say, and that if they didn't make me go back to Second Chance to finish the program then they would ultimately be letting me down. She stressed to them that I needed to complete the program for my own self-esteem. "Tough Love," I guess. I just can't see the appeal. The only thing about love that's tough is that it should be unconditional.

Seeing no other viable option that day, I sullenly walked with them out of the room, my back to Mr. Ed, down the corridor and out to the church parking lot to my parents' car. I knew if I ran, I would eventually be arrested and the unthinkable would happen; I'd be court mandated into Second Chance until I was twenty-one.

We rode the thirty minutes back to Second Chance with the senior staff member sitting in the back seat beside me. She asked me, gently, but several times, "Brian, what are you thinking about?" I silently cried.

When we reached Second Chance, early that Saturday afternoon, I walked on my own free will back into the group (still in dried, mud-caked clothes and socks) and sat in one of the pews. Everything got quiet for a minute while I was walking in. I'm sure everyone was wondering where I had been all day and why I was in such a disheveled state. The group quickly lost interest though and the rap started up again.

My oldcomer was sitting a pew away, clearly seething mad but happy I'd been caught. He was trying his hardest not to look at me. I tried to avoid eye contact with him as well. I didn't want to pour salt into the wound. About ten minutes later, Jean Cassidy came strolling in.

Mrs. Cassidy stopped group rap, stood me up, and called me out in front of everyone for about five minutes. She let everyone in the group shamefully know what I had done. I didn't say anything. What could I say? I could see some shock on some of the other programmers' and staff faces. Hardly anyone had run away from this place. To be back so quickly as well was very odd.

I sat through the rest of the afternoon and at home assignments was sent to a different, new host home. I was assigned to a 5th phaser, who had two other 5th phasers in tow. They let me know on the car ride home that they eagerly awaited me trying to run again.

In my oldcomer for the night's parents' car, three of us programmers crammed in the back, me in the middle and the oldcomer and his mom driving up front, I tried my best to reassure them that I had no intention of running. I was broken. My new oldcomer still gave me some horrible wedgies with the "hand of friendship" that night and throughout the next day.

Chapter 15
Sunday (chore day)

I woke up Sunday with all three of the oldcomers singing the horrible wake-up song to me. We ate breakfast at the oldcomer's house and then headed into the center. When we arrived at Second Chance, a lot of the first through fourth phase parents were there as well. Reverend Scotty led the service. He passionately intertwined Bible verses and Satan persuasively with our past taboo drug and alcohol use, which was, of course, the root of all our problems.

Shortly after the service, we same four went back home to our host parents' house for lunch. Then, hoping maybe I'd get a break, I found out I was sorely wrong. Sunday at Second Chance was "chore day."

For the next six or so hours, us programmers would complete a long list of chores around the house for the host parents. If we were lucky, the host parents would call it off after a few hours and play board games with us. Unlucky, we worked hard for six plus hours.

I, as happened on this particular day, was rarely lucky until, months later, when I got to go back to my parents' house on second phase and become an oldcomer myself. My parents were pretty chill about not working us all day long on Sunday, chore day. Most of the other programmers' parents, however, took full advantage of our free labor. I'm pretty certain a few houses I stayed at didn't own or believe in board games.

Chapter 16
Monday (run day)

That next morning, dark and early with that damn wake-up song ringing in my head, we went back to the center. The 3rd through 5th phasers left for school; my new oldcomer not forgetting to stand me up and challenge me before he left.

The staff leading the group also stood me up and challenged me for a minute at the beginning of the first rap. I guess I was still everyone's favorite toy. I didn't say much other than that I still didn't belong there and sat down.

Later in the morning, we had another intake happen to another poor soul. This one looked younger than me, maybe thirteen. The oldcomer set him down in the middle of the second pew, near me. The kid was unable to stop trembling and shaking.

He just sat there, quaking with eyes closed. He eventually started singing Metallica songs through the whole rap while ignoring all the staff and fifth phase programmers telling him to be quiet. He sang aloud for twenty minutes at least, belting out Metallica songs that dove into the concepts of captivity and being brainwashed. Everyone else was trying to ignore him, but I, for one, loved it. I thought it was genius at the time. I still do. He probably had the most love in his heart out of anyone in that group at that time.

When we stood to go to the bathroom before lunch, the nervous newcomer, who was in front of me in the single-file line, decided he was done, and it was time to make a break for it. With a quick jerking motion, he broke free of the oldcomer's "hand of friendship" and simultaneously sprinted forward.

The poor kid only made it twenty feet before two oldcomers twice his size rawdogged him, face first, into the carpet covered concrete floor. Then, two additional oldcomers sat on his legs and helped restrain them. Staff came over and critiqued the restraint.

The kid soon after cried "Uncle!" and staff had two of the oldcomers carry him, each holding a twisted arm behind the kid's back, out of the room and down the hall. So, now I know what happens when you try to run while you are in the center. Good to know.

Later that week, the unthinkable happened. A 5thphaser had run away in the middle of the night to see her old "druggie" friends. She was caught and now relegated to restart the program all over again. I think she was fourteen months in. She sat in group for several days, fuming just like me and the other new programmers. I definitely didn't blame her.

Chapter 17
Stuck with nowhere but up to go

After "sitting" most of the next week, I finally had the ultimate epiphany. One afternoon, while "in my head" during group, I realized I was stuck and had no real choices in front of me. I was in a cage with only one way out, doing the time and allowing them to mold me into what they wanted.

I vividly remember sitting in the pews during the group rap and going into a quiet psychotic break, trying to justify this personality shift I was about to undertake. I clearly visualized in my mind's eye two surfers riding on waves right above me. One of them looked down at me and said, "Don't worry Brian, chill. Just make some stuff up if you need to. We got you. You can survive this." That was the point when I decided to start making stuff up and tried to follow the program so that I could complete it in the shortest time possible. The only real choice I felt I had.

Suddenly, I pathetically started flapping my arms out in front of me. Staff, surprised almost as much as I was, immediately called my name. I slowly stood in group and started by getting "honest" and embellishing my drug list, so I sounded like everyone else there. I added crack cocaine, heroin, and a host of painkillers to my drug list. I got "honest" like they wanted. It was far from the truth.

The list of drugs just flowed out. I even surprised myself as I named them. Oddly, everyone else in group seemed to buy it. I guess my drug list was average in the group's minds. I mean, it wasn't as weird as one kid who had previously said one of his drugs on his list were dried banana peels. He tried to smoke them once, to no effect.

I made sure not to list banana peels. My dad would many years later confess to me that whenever that kid would list that in their druggie list on Friday nights, my dad was always confused because he didn't know you could get high on banana peels. My dad would always grin when telling the story. I think he was making a funny. You're right dad, you can't. Damn if that kid didn't try once out of boredom and sheer will so as to possibly experience good feelings.

I then shared with the group my story of the Friday night before I got sent to drug treatment, but this time greatly embellishing it. For example, I said that I had gone to the apartments in Collierville intending to get crack cocaine, and that I had brought it to the party, getting several of my friends high on crack for the first time and making a bunch of money.

That's when my waterworks started. Especially with how shitty I was feeling just "sitting." I had been so depressed that I had to let it out. I could tell most of the other kids bought my fabricated story, and my semi-honest tears.

Staff bought it for sure, and that was what was important. This was the first time I would get praise from staff; when I actually lied to them. I knew that there was no good way out, but I did see some sort of light at the end of the tunnel. I also knew for certain that there were people who had made it through this retched hellhole. It was only logical to me at the time that I could get through it as well. I could become who they wanted me to be. I could play the role.

So, I stopped sitting that day and started "working the program," as they say. The next couple of weeks involved me opening up more in group rap and making up more ridiculous stories and associated feelings.

The only physical exercise I would get most days was ten minutes of jumping jacks and push-ups in group in the morning and the afternoon. Sometimes, rarely, we would get fortunate, and a staff member would take us all out back to a small, chain-linked fence area for a little bit of outside time. Again, that was rare.

Home-schooling was a joke as well. Around three times a week, in the mornings for about an hour, we would get led into one of the separate conference rooms in the warehouse. There was always a retired teacher sitting there who would volunteer her time to watch us and answer any questions we might have when we read our assigned books. The assigned books were based off of the most recent classes we had taken in high school.

I remember, me being in second year Latin at the time, she gave me a book that taught Latin. However, she didn't know Latin, so I couldn't ask her any real questions. She just told me to read the book and try to answer the quizzes at the end of each chapter the best I could. The answers were in the back of our books, she never graded our quizzes, but we could ourselves. It was extremely hard to learn Latin through a book without a teacher or hearing the actual pronunciation of the dead language. We all miraculously received "A's" while at the center by the retired teacher, whether we did anything or not. Even if we did anything, no one was going to grade and correct it.

Chapter 18
The Key to Willingness
December 1991

A few weeks before Christmas, and a month into Second Chance, we held a group rap during the morning centering on "the key to willingness." The staff member led the rap by relating a Bible verse to one of the Alcohol Anonymous twelve-steps and having the willingness to open up to others. It was targeted towards those three or four of us 1st phasers that were "sitting" and not working the program. We made large skeleton keys out of paper and wrote applicable scripture verses on them. My oldcomer was not there; he was at school. I never discussed this with my oldcomer until after the key incident.

Later that night, after supper and on our way to share MI reports, my oldcomer led me alone into his living room by the "hand of friendship." While walking, we both heard a very loud thud on the ground to our left. We both turned, and lying on the ground, about a foot or two away, was a large brass skeleton key. It was approximately eight inches long.

I immediately shivered. My oldcomer quickly asked me how the hell I'd gotten a skeleton key? I just stammered and tried to explain that it wasn't mine. I then loudly exclaimed that I didn't know where it came from or what it went to. He was just as adamantly defiant to me that it wasn't his, and that he didn't believe me. His parents then came in and immediately started challenging me as well. It wasn't their key, nobody in the house had ever seen it before, they were all certain. Where did I get it from?

We eventually got through our MI reports for the night, and I again promised that I didn't know what that key was or where it came from, even though my MI report (written before the key apparition) was about the key to willingness rap and relating it to a past drug use story. They were even more suspicious after my report that night and turned the key over to staff the next morning.

That same next morning, a staff member stood me up in group and, holding the key out in her hand, asked me where it came from. I told her the truth, that I didn't know and last night was the first time I'd ever seen it. I got challenged a little bit in group that day about it as well.

When the 3rd through 5th phasers got back from school, I was challenged again in group, this time by my oldcomer and staff. I told them again it wasn't mine. I don't think they believed me.

To this day, my oldcomer and I are both adamant that we don't know where that key came from, what it goes to, or how it got dropped on the floor beside us while we were alone walking through his living room. Surely, we would have seen or felt someone else trying to do it?

If my oldcomer or his parents did do it, they're magicians. Also, if my oldcomer did it, he's a dick. He'd sworn to me that he didn't do it and knew nothing about the key, still insistent for many years later that he thought it was mine. We never saw the key again after that.

Regardless, whether it was a key thrown down on the ground by my oldcomer, a trap set by his parents and Second Chance, or an actual physical sign from The Almighty God; I got the hint. I figured if I was all in, then I needed to be all in.

After sleeping on it for a night or two, I found the willingness to share my terrible secret in a morning group rap session. It was more of a strategic move by me. I figured, if nothing else, that it would help with taking the focus off my drug and alcohol stories that I was embellishing, or flat out making up. At any rate, I could certainly cry at the drop of a pin thinking about it, and it would get me some sympathy points with staff, maybe speeding up my progression out of there.

My secret was that by the age of six, I had already been, and continued to be for two more years, sexually and physically abused by a male friend of the family. It was a regular occurrence. I know that seems physically young; but yes, not to overshare, I was already getting erections and dry orgasms by the age of five.

I remember feeling such shame at the time of the abuse. Not only because of the powerlessness I felt over what was happening, but also the pure physical enjoyment I felt while it was happening at such a young and naïve age.

It started off by us perusing male gay magazines that he had with him when nobody else was around. Quickly it advanced to giving and receiving fellatio and anal intercourse.

My abuser was a teenager whom I was terribly frightened of. He had already given me a black eye and a sprained wrist. He was easily three times my size. It was something I couldn't process at that age.

Shortly after me sharing my secret in group, where there were a lot of crying teens in the group sharing that they could relate to me, I was pulled out of group to come talk to an executive staff member.

She brought me into one of the small conference rooms off the hall, an oldcomer tightly gripping me on the "hand of friendship" the entire way, and, after the oldcomer sat me down in a chair, the staff member asked me if what I had just said in group was true. I said "yes" and spilled. It was nice to tell someone, anyone, what had happened after all of that time of holding it in. Even though I disliked both of those people at the time, they seemed sympathetic to my suffering.

Later that day, staff quietly gave me a Christian therapy book for survivors of sexual child abuse and told me I could read it whenever I wasn't in group. I would also start attending a special weekly group rap for the programmers in Second Chance who had also been previously sexually abused. I unfortunately don't remember ever getting any real help until many years later.

Those weekly sexual abuse raps I attended at the center ended up consisting of almost half of the programmers at Second Chance at the time, around twenty of us. I heard a lot of very tragic stories in those private group raps that I do believe were very true. It was very sad but gave me a little bit of hope at the same time. I realized I wasn't the only one trapped in this current situation, and, if someone who suffered more horrific abuse than I could advance in the program, then I surmised that I had a shot as well. That's the thing about survivors, they're contagious.

Not that I had a whole lot of options at the time. But, hey, I didn't want to kill myself. I wasn't willing to give up on this game called life. Fortunately, I've never really liked the thought of concession, although I've had the thoughts many times. I'm not trying to shame my friends that have committed suicide, I understand their internal struggle. It's really fucking hard to keep going when you have fucked up shit happen to you. I just never liked the idea of intentionally hurting my loved ones. I saw the aftermath of my mom's family's devastation when they lost a loved one to suspected suicide. Devastate is probably too kind of a word to use.

Shortly after deciding to work the program at Second Chance, I experienced my first Christmas without my parents. I would like to think I made the most of it. I like making lemonade out of lemons. My host parents were nice. We watched "It's a Wonderful Life" at their home on Christmas Eve and listened to Christmas songs afterwards. I think they got me a dress shirt that I could wear at Second Chance as a gift.

Second Chance also gave me some new church clothes that my parents had bought for me to wear at the center. Buttoned-up collared shirts with black slacks. I think I also got a new toothbrush and sanitary items from them.

I remember wishing for a Christmas miracle that somehow my parents would find the will to pull me from the program. That's what's called "wishful thinking." My parents were trapped, along with everyone else the Cassidys had snared into their expansive and money-making web. Nothing but coal in my stockings that year.

Chapter 19
A New Year
January 1992

Shortly after the New Year of my fifteenth year on this planet, Scotty announced in front of all programmers before Friday night rap that I had advanced to the first rank of first phase, Talk. My first promotion. Everyone applauded. I was elated, my acting was actually working.

There was more applause to be had when the Friday night rap crowd later found out. Parents loved to see promotions at Second Chance; it reinforced the 95% success rate idea and the $10,000 or so they wasted on the shithole of a place.

My parents were very proud of me. They told me so on the microphone. After the Friday night rap, I got to sit with them in one of the back pews for a timed ten minutes due to my new responsibility/promotion. An oldcomer sat right beside me.

It was a pretty quiet conversation except for my mom trying to constantly fill me in on family things. The oldcomer interrupted her at least five times, asking her to please not "talk behind backs." The few words my dad said included letting me know, again, that he was proud of me for deciding to work on myself. Both of my parents encouraged me to continue working the program so that I could come home. I remember being shocked at the time that they already knew the Second Chance lingo. It dawned on me at that moment they were being brainwashed as well.

Chapter 20
Talk & Responsibility

The next couple of weeks at Second Chance started to go a little smoother for me. I had learned what staff and the other teens wanted me to do when standing up in group rap: tell a story of a time where I used drugs and alcohol, explain how it negatively affected me and those around me, and explain how I felt thinking about it while hopefully shedding a tear or two. I saw the equation and answer to this particular madness that was ruining my life.

Now, again, I had maybe one story I could possibly shed tears about, and that's only if I falsely added crack cocaine into it and got all my good friends, including my best friend (who wasn't even at the party), high; ruining their lives as well. I could cry over that. Though untrue as it was, it was close enough to the truth to illicit major feelings.

After that story was a success in group, I decided to start making up stories in my head that I could somehow see myself doing if I was the most miserable piece of shit teen version of myself to walk the earth. I would later find out that most of the stories the other teens told were also about 75% embellished. They weren't the miserable piece of shits that they portrayed themselves to be either. We were acting in order to survive.

In case you're wondering, the reason why we all did this was because we needed to cry in group while telling our stories or we would get "challenged" and not advance. We also had to convince staff and the other programmers that we weren't "faking." If we kept telling the same two stories, we would get challenged. We had to have at least ten past drug use incidents always on rotation when we were called on to share in group. We just had to stick to our embellished stories and not get caught changing details. It was an art form that we all had to learn in order to progress in the program.

As the weeks progressed, I slowly got much better at acting and figuring out this program's formula. I was determined to graduate the program in the shortest time possible. I was going for a record.

I would find out later that a lot of the programmers were initially scared to be my friend because I had become such a "good doer," and they were afraid I was going to rat them out if they broke any rules. Damned if I do, damned if I don't.

Within a month I had risen to T&R (Talk and Responsibility) and could finally be let off the "hand of friendship." Instead, an oldcomer would delicately hold on to the back of my shirt while I walked. Thank God, no more wedgies!

Chapter 21
Second phase (coming home)
March 1992

I had no real setbacks over the next couple of months. I even learned how to successfully challenge the other programmers daily in group rap. I was starting to "get it."

One Friday, during Scotty's weekly announcements, I finally heard the promotion I had been waiting for, "Brian Q. is going home."

It was so corny too. In Friday night rap, when my parents would get the microphone, oblivious to what was coming, I was supposed to yell "coming home!" and run over to them, giving them a hug. I always envisioned, but never saw anyone brazen enough, at that point for them to keep running, yelling "Fuck you everyone!" over their shoulders while they jetted out the side emergency exit.

What happened instead was that I yelled "coming home" and ran to my parents in tears for a hug. After Friday night rap, and my "coming home" announcement, I got to meet my parents out in the parking lot with a fifth phase oldcomer there to supervise us for the night. I kept having to remind my parents about the program rules because my mom couldn't stop talking behind backs to catch me up on what was going on with family and friends. She had a really hard time with that rule.

My mom tried to follow it though, bless her heart. She knew if she didn't, she'd get stood up at the next parent group rap by executive staff and challenged for about five minutes on it, risking my progress in the program. So, needless to say, the ride home that night was very awkward with me repeating to her things like, "no mom, you can't say your co-worker's name or let me know how she's doing, she's not here right now."

That night, when we arrived at my parents' home in Collierville, it was the first time I had seen the house in almost six months. I was so happy to be home. However, I realized that it was still a cage.

There were a million things I couldn't do. I couldn't go outside, not even in the backyard; I still couldn't listen to media, of any kind, not even Christian; and the only thing I could read at home was the Bible, the Alcoholic Anonymous Big Book, and the sexual abuse book Second Chance had given me.

Still, it was nice to be back inside of the smell of my parents' home.

While I was gone, my childhood bedroom that was upstairs had been stripped clean and all of my old stuff had disappeared. I would find out later that an executive staff member went through all of my stuff with my parents before I came home and threw out all of it. They also threw away a large box of Grateful Dead stuff, including a lot of original bootleg cassette tapes. Everything, gone, in the trash. All of my poetry, music, books, posters, and musings.

I didn't care too much at the time. It took about five years for it to fully dawn on me what all I had lost that was meaningful to me; it was invaluable. I later realized I would have rather Second Chance stab me directly into my heart and gotten it over with. But at the time, I was just glad to be home.

Second Chance staff also wouldn't let me back in my old bedroom upstairs. Instead, my parents had to convert their downstairs guest bedroom. They had moved everything out and added two twin beds. There was nothing in the bedroom; except for the beds, sleeping bags, pillows and blankets, a Bible, an alarm clock (no radio), a brand-spanking new pee jug, and alarms on the doors and windows.

My parents would later add a third twin bed once it became apparent that Second Chance wasn't going to let me be at home alone and kept sending at least two other boys to stay with me every night.

I didn't try to kill myself then. To be honest, I'm not sure why. In retrospect, I think there were a plethora of intertwined reasons why I didn't want to check out. The largest being that I wasn't willing to concede.

I'm glad that most of the programmers at the time also didn't concede and marched on through the madness of life. They were beautiful kids with beautiful souls. None of us deserved what was happening to us at the time. Somehow, against all odds, a lot of them have become very beautiful adults with beautiful kids that also have beautiful souls.

I was suddenly very careful not to break any rules that night. I did not want to start the next five months over. I also didn't want to get challenged by the 5th phaser staying with me when we went back to the center the next morning. Luckily, this oldcomer was cool, and he didn't challenge me on any of my slip ups, minor as they were. I guess he could tell I was trying.

I would almost always have another programmer come home with me for the next year, usually out-of-towners that needed a host house to stay for the night. It seemed that just as soon as I got used to sharing my bedroom with someone, they were moved to a different host home.

Even though the pee jug smell would burn my nostrils through the nights, I still felt like a prince when I came home each day after all day group raps at Second Chance. I could sleep in my own bed.

My usual routine for the next year was coming home from the center at night, writing my MI report of the day, eating a home-cooked meal, and then MI report discussion with my parents and whoever else from Second Chance happened to be there for the night.

We always went to bed shortly after, sometimes before the sun went down.

I also felt like a newly coronated prince at Second Chance due to my newfound oldcomer status as well. I could put newcomers on the "hand of friendship," was able to tackle anyone if they tried to run away, and, since most of the 3rd through 5th phasers were at school, I felt the terrifying thrill of authority in group during the day; however self-perceived it was.

I had also learned how to hone my acting skills in daily group raps as well. I occasionally made a few mishaps. We all made mishaps.

You knew you were in trouble if someone started flapping their arms during the middle of a story you were telling in group rap. That usually meant they were motivated about something and probably up to no good. Sure enough, staff would call on them, and the overzealous programmer would stand up and say, as challengingly as they could, "Brian, I challenge you on your story right now. Where are your feelings? Are you being honest?"

Not wanting to be actually honest and start the discipline cycle all over again, I would turn to look at the staff leading the group rap to see if they had a concerned look on their faces and reply back with what I had seen work with others: "I'm sorry, I'm not feeling well," and then, while turning to the staff and rest of group, I would swear that "I really was feeling my story and those are my real feelings."

If I was lucky, the staff leading the group wouldn't negatively mark me down in their logbook and nobody else would challenge me. Unlucky, and I would get challenged for the next thirty minutes by the group until I really did cry.

Of course, the challenging of someone while they were sharing a story in group was a double-edged sword and very risky. Sometimes staff would believe the person telling the story and challenge the challenger. The staff member would get upset that the challenger had interrupted the storyteller while they were honestly sharing openly in rap. Then, instead of the normal reward of getting a positive notation in the staff logbook, staff would negatively notate the challenger for not being empathetic. They would then get challenged for a while in group.

Challenging others during group rap storytelling was chancy, and really depended on the staff member leading the group and their opinion of the storyteller's performance. It was a suspenseful and twirlingly upsetting dance.

I'm not sure how the same staff member ever used to lie about their own stories when they were in the program, and then not be able to spot lies in others later, but I would guess it was a combination of empathy and lying about their stories for so long that they become truths, even to themselves. Plus, I'm sure getting paid didn't hurt.

For the next few months, my second phase zoomed along. I usually had oldcomers from out-of-town stay with me, but, rarely, I would be assigned to be home alone with my parents. Later, once I started having newcomers, I would find out how rare an occasion it was to be alone while in Second Chance.

Even when I had the chance to be alone though, I wouldn't break the rules. The fear of my parents catching me and having to start all over was a terrifying prospect. At least I could fix myself a lunch from home now if I wanted. Oh, I wanted. It became my life mission to never eat that left-over slop the center got from Central Church anytime, ever again, unless absolutely necessary.

I occasionally had an out-of-town oldcomer who would have an out-of-town newcomer in tow. It was an odd experience and was how I was trained to have a newcomer. The oldcomer always made a point to challenge the newcomer as often as they could.

Chapter 22

The exorcism

One weekday on second phase, while the 3rd thru 5th phasers were in school, Mrs. Cassidy walked into group late that morning and said to us, "Brian Q., would you please grab a specific newcomer by the hand of friendship and line up against the wall." I immediately did as she requested.

She then called out seven other oldcomer names, three boys and four girls, and told all nine of us to follow her. We trailed her down the hall, my newcomer in tow, and walked into one of the conference rooms used for school.

In that small conference room, Mrs. Cassidy had already set up a circle of ten metal folding chairs. She pointed and told me to put my newcomer down in a chair opposite from her. I was to sit beside him, and then she directed the rest of the oldcomers to sit in the rest of the seats and all of us to hold each other's hands. We formed a circle, with Mrs. Cassidy completing it in the tenth chair upfront. She allowed a few oldcomers of different genders to hold hands in order to complete the circle.

Mrs. Cassidy then thanked all of us for joining her and said that, as oldcomers and shining knights of the Lord, we had a Christian duty and obligation to participate in what was about to happen that day. Apparently, the newcomer that I had brought with me on the "hand of friendship" was possessed by an evil demon and needed group prayer to drive that demon out of him. We were here, under her Holy guidance, to exorcise his demon away through group prayer.

For the next twenty minutes we, as a group with Mrs. Cassidy leading us, prayed as hard as we could, mostly out loud while not interrupting someone else. We prayed and prayed, willing the devil out of the newcomer. He just sat there, giggling occasionally when I'd try to reach out for his hand, slapping mine away. When he giggled it just motivated us to try and pray even harder.

Eventually, after about twenty minutes of this and the newcomer going quiet just out of sheer boredom and exhaustion, Mrs. Cassidy declared the exorcism as being complete and a success. The newcomer snickered. She then thanked us all for joining our first exorcism and for helping. We filed out, while I picked up the newcomer on the "hand of friendship." He was still giggling his ass off when we got back to group.

After some time on second phase, I was assigned my very own newcomer with an oldcomer in tow. I think I played the part of the oldcomer pretty well. I was a nice oldcomer, just very strict when it came to the rules. I wasn't going to let anyone set me back if I could help it. I wanted out of this hellhole as quickly as possible.

Over the next few months, I continued being an exemplary 2nd phaser. I was assigned more newcomers and continued to work on my program in the center during the day, trying my best not to get challenged in group. I occasionally would be assigned at nights to go to other host homes and help them with their newcomers, but, for the most part, I was usually assigned to go home with other programmers at my house. I always felt bad for my parents when they later would tell me they had been waiting for me in the parking lot to go home and staff informed them that I was going to help out at another host home. That had to have been hard.

Chapter 23
Third phase
June 1992

Eventually, I advanced to the third phase. Fairly quickly as well seeing that I had zero demotions from then on. Summer had just started, so that meant I wouldn't be able to go to Germantown High for a couple of months. Also, since I wasn't on fourth or fifth phase yet, I had to stay in the center all day with the rest of the programmers. This meant that there wasn't much of a change for me except that I could read more approved (mainly Christian-based) literature.

I've always been a voraciously hungry reader, and my parents did luckily gift me several Christian fantasy novels at that time. The novels were mainly about various guardian angels coming down to Earth and vanquishing evil doers. I enjoyed them, wondering where my angels were.

On one hot summer afternoon prior to home assignments, Mrs. Cassidy came in and said, twang and all, "now, listen up group. I know that we rarely allow anyone to talk behind anyone's backs, but we have a special person that we are intaking today. His name is Rob, and several months ago, while taking LSD, Rob tried to end his life. It has left him physically deformed. The reason I say this is because I don't want anyone to be alarmed and everyone to openly welcome him."

Shortly after, a very scared Rob was led into group by the "hand of friendship" from a staff person who sat him down in the middle of the boys' side second row pew. Rob had a white towel wrapped around the entire lower portion of his head, up to the bottom of his eye sockets.

Since my mom was a nurse, I was assigned Rob as my newcomer, and Rob came home with us along with a 5th phaser for the night. On the drive home, we got to hear Rob's harrowing story, reader beware.

A few months prior, Rob, who was eighteen, was hanging out with his younger brother and friends at their mom's house. Somehow, they had gotten a hold of some blotter LSD acid through friends and decided to try it.

Now, blotter acid is blotting paper that has been impregnated with pure LSD liquid (a.k.a. acid). The paper absorbs the liquid in suspension until you place the piece of paper in your mouth. The big problem with this is that you never really know how much or what is on the blotter paper. One square could be one dose or ten doses depending on the strength. It could also be mixed with something a little more sinister like PCP.

There's no way of really knowing what or how much Rob ingested.

So, after ingesting the supposed LSD blotter paper and starting to feel its effects, Rob decided it was a good idea to show off his father-in-law's hunting shotgun to his younger brother and friends. They were in the living room watching television, parents away at work, when Rob brought the shotgun out. He sat down with it in a chair, and not being in control of his senses, put the shotgun under his chin while announcing to the room in a playful manner "hey, look, I'm going to blow my brains out."

No one knows, including Rob himself, if he meant to pull that trigger. He certainly had reasons to want to do so, but I'm not sure if he meant to. However, the gun went off, and Rob lost the bottom half of his face.

His upper palate and nasal structure stopped the shotgun pellets from making it to his brain. Instead, it shredded the bottom portion of his face, completely removing his lower jaw; taking months of surgery to get him to the point where he could wear a towel around the bottom half of his head and drink through a straw.

My mom would make different types of nutrition shakes for him for breakfast, lunch at Second Chance, and dinner. Rob shared his story with the entire group once, later, during his first week. After hearing the story, an obviously true one, neither the staff nor anyone else were really willing to challenge him.

Chapter 24

Runaway

About a week or so into his treatment, I could tell that Rob was not digging this program. He was eighteen, and, after his court-ordered short-term therapy while in the hospital, he was remanded into his mom's care until he was twenty-one. She somehow had been given the Second Chance spiel while he was in the hospital, probably that same damn brochure, and was convinced this was the best place for him.

Rob was not happy. I didn't blame him. It was very awkward that week asking him "what are you thinking about?" while at home. I would try it as gently and meagerly as I could. He would never answer. I would never repeat the question after the first try each night. 5th phasers kept coming home with me as well and were also very reluctant to press Rob.

Rob was a complete sweetheart though and had an extremely bright soul. You could see it in his eyes and feel it radiate from him. Even with all of his hurt and anger, he was extremely nice to me and often joked.

We played Legos and board games that Sunday of his first week with my parents and had a really good time. I was trying to be as compassionate as I could be. No way was I going to challenge Rob at home or in group rap unless he did something major.

One evening on the ride home, about a week or so into his being at Second Chance, I could tell that Rob was extremely anxious and planning something. He was quiet the whole ride home while sitting in the middle, between me and an oldcomer (a 5th phaser that used to be my oldcomer), in the back seat. His right leg was rhythmically shaking. I just thought he was upset though. I didn't think that he was going to try and make a break for it.

We rolled into my parents' garage, my dad driving, and parked. I started gently applying the "hand of friendship" to Rob and loosely guided him out of the backseat. Suddenly Rob bolted. My grip was too loose, and he popped right out of it. Out the garage door Rob ran.

The 5th phaser and I both caught up and tackled him in my front yard, having to restrain him on the ground. Luckily it was soft grass, and we were able to wrap Rob up in a restraint hold before he got hurt.

A jogger going by at that moment had a very confused look on her face when she happened to see this. She briefly stopped on the paved suburban neighborhood street, clearly stunned at what she had just seen, but then she just kept on jogging. My parents called the chain of command local contact sheet for Second Chance host parents, while we sat there for ten minutes trying to restrain Rob in my front lawn without seriously hurting him.

We finally got Rob to settle down. Defeated, he let us take him back into the house. Another 5th phaser who lived nearby came by shortly later for physical support in case Rob tried to run again. I don't know if I've ever felt sadder for someone, nor so mad at myself for the situation I was put in.

Rob was removed from group the next day by Mrs. Cassidy, barely a word, no oldcomer needed. He didn't return. He wasn't assigned to me, or anyone else that night. I never saw him again.

To this day I don't know how he was able to get out. I pray that his mom finally saw the light and pulled him out. I hope she didn't lose her $10,000; but she may have. If she borrowed to pay the admittance fee, she probably lost a lot more.

I hope Rob found the real help he needed. He was such a kind and gentle soul. He definitely didn't belong in Second Chance. He needed a real second chance, as most of us do. I pray he got it.

Chapter 25
Back to school
September 1992

The long and grueling summer before my junior year of high school finally came and went. I was so happy to start school. I wasn't sure what to expect, but I reckoned that anything would beat sitting in that hot warehouse in group raps all day. I was really nervous though. I remember thinking "what if someone I know tries to talk to me?" The "what if's" went dancing merrily in my head, completely unchecked. At that time, Second Chance had even convinced me that I was going to have to turn down drug offers by other students every five minutes. I was scared as all get out.

However, weighing the risks vs. sitting in group, I got the courage that first morning of my junior year of high school to ask a 5th phaser to be excused and walked towards my carpool ride to freedom, or what was freedom for me at the time. Elated to be able to skip most of the daily group rap sessions, I jumped into the host parent's car (the parents took turns each morning) with the rest of the Germantown High designated kids. The number ranged from six to ten of us at any given time and was usually split between two vehicles separating the boys from girls.

Germantown High School was about fifteen minutes away and a medium-sized school at that time by Memphis standards. It totaled a little less than 2,000 students in 1992. The town of Germantown, Tennessee was a wealthy suburb of Memphis. The high school was where a lot of the students with rich parents, who couldn't for some reason or another go to private school, would attend. It was a Southern version of Beverly Hills 90210.

I had previously seen numerous challenges in group by other programmers who had "caught" another programmer breaking the rules at school. This included being demoted all the way back to first phase, as was the case with one programmer who was busted for smoking a cigarette with an old "druggie friend" in the school's parking lot.

To put it plainly, we were greatly encouraged to snitch on each other, and, since we weren't sure where the other programmers were at any given time in the school, we didn't want to be busted and so followed all of the rules and then some.

Luckily, for my own peace of mind, I was never in a situation where I felt that I really needed to snitch on anyone. No matter what minor rule I might have thought they were breaking. Now, If I'd seen physical or sexual abuse by a programmer to or by someone else, well, then that would have been a different story.

Also, I wanted out of Second Chance really badly. Really, really badly. No way I was breaking a single fucking Second Chance rule at school. I had grand delusions that I could still make my senior prom.

My high school experience as a "Second Chance kid" started out the typical way for any junior starting high school in a completely new town. No one knew me, not unsurprisingly. I did, however, get a lot of people suddenly asking me the time. Dressed in church clothes sans tie, the only other accessory I could have, other than a belt, was a watch.

That watch got me in a lot of trouble. It seemed like almost everyone loved to ask me the time at Germantown High that first month. The first day was hilarious. I kept spouting out "I can't talk to you, I'm in drug rehab," they would give me a very weird look, and then I'd walk away with my head down. It was what Second Chance told me I had to say if anyone at school tried to talk to me. I guess answering the time of day could lead to drug use somehow? Moments later, I'd have another kid approach me in the hallway and ask me for the time.

I get it. I was in church clothes with a watch; who else in the school halls to reliably ask the time from? I don't think most of the Germantown High School kids were picking on me, but I'm certain they were confused by my response that first month. I'm glad no one ever hit me. It came close though.

A couple of weeks into my junior year at Germantown High, I was sitting at my desk in history class reading the Bible, the teacher gone to run an errand and allowing us free time, when, suddenly, I felt some very large fingers tapping my shoulder. I thought it was an adult, but it wasn't. I turned around and, instead, loomed a huge teenager, all muscle, much taller and bigger than me. He stood towering over me with a gloomy and serious face. He wore a Germantown football letter jacket. He was at least twice as thick as me and had me beat in height and arm reach by a couple of inches.

He then asked me, I believe once again, based on the agitated look on his face, although I didn't hear him the first time, "what time is it?" I, without thinking, spouted out "I can't talk to you, I'm in drug rehab."

I could tell from his reaction as soon as those words left my mouth that I had made a very grave error. I reckoned it's the same reaction I'd get if I'd kicked his dog. He wasn't having any of that.

So, me sitting at my desk, on the verge of being pummeled into oblivion, had an angel come down from somewhere, out of nowhere. A student a couple of desks away said, "Hey, he's in Second Chance." The football player turned toward her with a confused look on his face. She then said, "He's in that drug rehab. Second Chance that won't let him talk to people; he could get in serious trouble if he talks to you."

The guy's face went from anger to sympathy in less than a second. He glanced down and saw I was reading the Bible and horror crept across his face. He turned to me and immediately apologized. I was floored and grateful the guy hadn't snapped me like a twig. I tried to give him the friendliest, most sincere, and grateful smile I could give. He turned around and walked to the back of the classroom to join his friends.

After that encounter, I soon stopped saying the phrase "I can't talk to you, I'm in drug rehab." when people asked me what time it was at Germantown High. I, instead, always told them the time. It was definitely a self-preservation move in my opinion, challenge in group be damned. I carefully navigated my way through Germantown High that year not talking to anyone except for other Second Chance programmers, teachers in class, or telling students the time. Yes, it was really fucking hard. We weren't even allowed to see the high school counselor.

Going back to group at Second Chance for afterschool rap was tricky as well. I tried a few different times to see if flapping my arms at a different rate resulted in my chances of getting "called on" less. I could never find a correlation. Staff always seemed to sense when I didn't want to get called on.

Us 3rd through 5th phasers were quick to be called on and quick to fold, seeing as we'd been in school all day. The challenge sharks would always circle during afterschool rap. Woe to those in group that they would see flailing. I saw newcomers who hadn't been there a week take part in after school group challenges when someone broke a rule at school. Most everyone in group would become outraged and deeply concerned.

Chapter 26
Fourth phase
October 1992

My sixteenth birthday came and went. No party, of course. We didn't celebrate birthdays at Second Chance for some reason. Maybe the cost of cake?

My parents did give me something though, a new $30 dress watch. Just what I needed. Thanks mom and dad. My parents also gave me a birthday cake, which I think is something all humans should have if possible on their birthday. I absolutely love birthday cake.

I continued to "work the program" that fall and, late one Friday in October, the Reverend Cassidy finally called my name for promotion to fourth phase. I'll be damned, which I feel I had the right to think at the time, I was going to finally get to hear music (albeit Christian) and watch approved television again.

Most television shows and PG-and-under rated movies were approved for 4th and 5th phasers and parents, but I do vividly remember the Cassidy's making a huge stink about no one watching "Married with Children" during a Friday night rap. That was not appropriate television in their minds.

In hindsight, I wouldn't be surprised if the Cassidy's secretly watched every episode of that show. Outwardly telling one another that they were watching it for informational purposes while silently enjoying the hell out of it. I could never watch television at home, except on rare occasions, because I usually had an oldcomer on a lower phase and/or a newcomer in the home with me.

I remember feeling extremely happy that night though. G and PG rated movies at the time were slim pickings, however I'd happily watch "The Land Before Time" for the 1,000th time if need be. I wasn't going to turn that down just to sit and stare at the wallpaper. I would happily watch and listen to anything "appropriate" you put in front of me. I'd been staring at the wallpaper for a year.

More importantly, I could request a weekly visit with my parents to the Christian bookstore or any other pre-approved place. When I was younger, my dad occasionally took my brother and myself, at my insistence, to a used paperback bookstore in Memphis. It was a small bookstore next to our barbershop that had cheap used books. God, I loved that bookstore smell. I usually finished a book as a child in the car before we even made it home.

I would love it if Paul McCartney came on the radio while I was reading in the backseat of my dad's car on the ride home. No matter what I was reading, his songs made it better.

But I couldn't listen to Paul McCartney at Second Chance. I could only listen to Christian music. It still had bars and a timestamp. Some kind of melody and beat. So, recreational music and movies were back in my rotation. I was happy.

Chapter 27
Christian music

There wasn't really too much of a difference between third and fourth phase while in the warehouse or at school, except for one odd thing...

While riding to school with my group that Monday after getting promoted, everyone in the van started getting really excited on the way out of the Second Chance parking lot to school. They begged the host parent to play a Christian cassette tape one of them had on them. Apparently, I had finally made it to fourth phase, and, since there were no other 3rd phasers in the van, we could listen to Christian music. Sweet freedom. Other than a few Christmas songs, I hadn't heard professionally recorded music in forever.

It also dawned on me at the time that I'd always been a deterrent the month before when I was with this group. I felt sad that I'd deprived them of music on their rides to and from school.

That only lasted for a couple of weeks before a programmer from second phase got promoted to third phase. No more Christian music on the rides to and from school for a little while. That's cool, at least someone got promoted to third phase.

It didn't matter to me. I'd already memorized all of the Christian artists' names that I liked. I knew what I could listen to at home now on my Walkman without getting challenged by any 4th and 5th phasers, or my parents. I felt legit. I now had something to ask my parents for, Christian music cassette tapes.

I quickly became addicted to Christian music. I knew every popular artist that proscribed to the Christian genre. Some were actually kind of good. Some sampled the hell out of mainstream artists whom I hope got paid. I haven't listened to much Christian music since my time in Second Chance.

Chapter 28
The Far Side

By the time fall of 1992 was in full swing, I was slipping into the character that Second Chance wanted me to be. I came very close to drinking Second Chance's Kool-Aid a couple of times and diving permanently into madness.

I remember admonishing myself when slipping into a rock song while doing menial tasks like chores. An inappropriate song would come sneaking into my head, and I'd say to myself "Stop singing negative songs Brian, get out of your head." I became really scared when I started believing in my own inner challenges.

I was teetering on the brink of insanity. I knew my creativity was almost completely sapped out of me. I was becoming a withered, hollowed-out stump of my old self. I had almost completely lost my identity.

I think I probably would have gone entirely dead in the brain if it wasn't for one book series that I was allowed to read for some reason, "The Far Side" comics by Gary Larson. It allowed me to laugh at something "appropriately." I couldn't be challenged in group over reading it, and it was extremely creative.

A couple of kids at Second Chance had picked up on this as well. We studiously read it. Every chance we got.

I quickly started making up and drawing my own "Far Side" comics. Completely appropriate, completely printable, but completely lost. What wasn't luckily lost was my creativity. Thank you, Mr. Larson. Thank you, creativity. If not for these things, I might have slipped away permanently into coo-coo land.

Another saving grace was that I discovered the Memphis Botanical Gardens on my weekly day off from group. Since I was able to go on outings once a week after school with my parents and then go home with them instead of returning to the center, I usually chose to go to the gardens with my mom.

The botanical gardens consisted of several acres of pure natural bliss that allowed me to reconnect back to nature. It even had a large Japanese koi pond, which I loved so very much. There was nothing more peaceful to me at the time than watching the extremely colorful koi fish or reading a Christian fantasy book about angels underneath a cherry tree.

I finally felt halfway sane for a brief moment on those outings. Someone else would usually take care of my newcomer for the night so I didn't even have to return to the Second Chance center until the next day.

I would occasionally go to the movie theater on my day's off with my dad. He also took me to a respectable pool hall a couple of times. He loved playing pool, and I loved playing it with him. It's a tradition we've continued throughout our lives.

Chapter 29
Thanksgiving
November 1992

Deep into fall, Thanksgiving rolled in. I was so appreciative at the time to finally be home for Thanksgiving that year. Things were going fairly smoothly for me. I rarely got challenged in group, and, if I did, I knew how to act my way out of it. Of course, I never intentionally broke the rules, so that helped as well. Every now and then I would slip off into a random rock song in my head, usually during chores, and then feel guilty. I was such a rebellious sixteen-year-old. Shame on me.

My mom went all out for Thanksgiving that year. I had a happy newcomer and out-of-town oldcomer with me for Thanksgiving dinner at our house. We ate well.

I did honestly feel grateful for my parents. I had started to sense that they had been ensnared by the Cassidy's web as much as I had and couldn't escape. My Spidey senses weren't wrong at the time. I just couldn't do anything about it.

I would find out later, as soon as they had let me go during my initial intake, my parents immediately regretted it. However, one of the executive staff members kept ensuring them at the time that everything was going to be fine and that I was in good hands, "in God's hands." My parents acquiesced and left. They didn't want to be the "bad" parents who pulled their son out of drug treatment before he got help, did they? It was a lot for them to take in at the time, and they were in an extremely vulnerable state. Shame on Second Chance. Shame.

They would also later tell me that they had to go to parents' afternoon rap several times a week where they, and the other parents, would challenge each other just like we did in group. One of the Cassidys was almost always leading the parents' group, and they would describe it as "brutal." The parents, like us programmers, were not allowed to talk about anyone who wasn't in the room with the other parents unless they were talking about their own child during group rap sharing.

So, it made it very hard to organize with the other parents and make a group consensus that Second Chance was wrong, even though my mom was certain that most of the other parents wanted to yank their children out of the program as well. They just could never fully talk to each other about it, nor reaffirm to each other the madness that was ensuing at the time.

There were many other tactics used for us "programmers" that were also modified for the parents. Guilt and fear were the most frequent motivating tools used. My mom later said that she and my dad had even thought about pulling me out on my sixteenthbirthday, but that they were too afraid to because of all of the great progress I had made. She said it also didn't help that executive staff made weekly, if not more, threats to the parents; reminding them that I would relapse and become a drug user on the streets if they pulled me from the program before I completed it.

Chapter 30
Fifth phase
December 1992

By the time winter of 1992 was in full-swing, Reverend Cassidy announced to the group at Friday promotions that I had made fifth phase. I was thrilled; that was a quick advancement through fourth phase. Just this last phase to go!

One of my new fifth phase privileges included being able to stand up on the side of the group during raps and answer other programmers' imperative questions quietly on the side of the pews. If a programmer had to immediately go to the bathroom, they would raise their hand halfway to their shoulder, and I would now have the authority to decide if it was an emergency or not. I, along with a few other 5th phasers, oversaw the boys' side of the pews.

I also now had two days off, which meant I could go somewhere with my parents twice a week after school, skipping the after-school raps, and then going back home with them. My parents usually split the duties. One parent (usually my mom) would take me to the gardens, or, if the weather wasn't cooperating, to a PG-rated movie at the movie theater and then home. The other parent (usually my dad) would have to go to Second Chance after work and pick up any out-of-town oldcomers, with usually newcomers in tow, from the center. Sometimes I'd have to go back to the center on my day off with my parents to pick up programmers for the night.

Another privilege was that I could now get my driver's learner's permit from the DMV on one of my days off, if my parents would allow it, and I would be able to drive with one of them in the passenger seat.

I politely begged my parents, and they took me to the DMV to get a permit. I was finally able to legally get behind the steering wheel of a car.

It took a while before my dad felt comfortable enough to let me drive when there were other programmers in the car. I remember one day on the ride home I didn't check my blind spot before getting over into the right lane. There were two programmers in the back seat.

Luckily, I made the lane transition slowly, and the other driver was paying attention. They honked while speeding safely away. Unfortunately for my right arm, my dad "frogged" me right away while scolding me. I have been very respectful of my blind spots from that point on while driving.

I was also finally able to skip Sunday service at Second Chance and go to church with my parents. However, I wasn't allowed by the Cassidys to go back to any churches in Collierville because I might run into old "druggie friends." A "druggy friend" was considered anyone I used to know in my past that was under the age of twenty-one and could sometimes include adults. It didn't matter if I used drugs with them or not. Second Chance's litmus test that they would tell us in group is that if that person makes you even think about who you were before Second Chance, then you were not allowed to talk to them and to avoid them at all costs.

Many programmers were demoted during my time there if they got caught talking to their old "druggie friends." I couldn't even reach out to my old Methodist Youth Fellowship church friends. My parents and I would usually end up going to Central Church on Sundays while I was on fifth phase in Second Chance.

So, I could miss group twice after school and on Sundays. It was progress. I was getting there, but I still had a ways to go.

Chapter 31
Christmas play
December 1992

I was a 5th phaser come Christmas, and very grateful for that opportunity and status at the time. I very clearly remembered where I was a year prior and did not want to go back there. I was willing to do whatever it took to get out of this hellhole and rejoin humanity.

Each Christmas was a big deal for everyone at Second Chance. We would spend several weeks rehearsing a Nativity play to be put on in front of the parents during a special Christmas gathering (usually on a Saturday). The honor of being in the play was always bestowed upon oldcomers that were "working their program." We got to skip group raps, a lot, for several weeks. Every time we were in the center, we were being pulled out of group rap to rehearse with one of the staff.

The Cassidys selected me to be Joseph, Jesus Christ's stepfather, a lead role in the play. Hallelujah, a Christmas miracle; I would have some break from the relentless challenging and drama of the group raps. I was starting to feel like I could breathe a little again. Slowly but surely things were looking up.

The Christmas Nativity play went off without a hitch, as boring as ever, and I worked my way into the New Year, thinking I would surely graduate in the next month or two.

Chapter 32
New Year 1993

The New Year rolled in, and I was ecstatic. I had just been picked for one of the lead roles in the Christmas play and hadn't been challenged in group in ages. The kid they picked last year for Joseph had graduated the next month. Was January to be my month?

I would find out later through my parents that I hadn't a snowball's chance in hell to graduate any time soon. My home was too good of a foster home, and the Cassidys didn't have the oldcomer numbers to release me at that time. They were bloated with 1st and 2nd phasers. The word had gotten out about Second Chance's success rate and the number of intakes each week continued to increase. Fifth phase would ultimately become my longest phase and last six months.

My mom later told me that she eventually challenged Reverend Cassidy after a parents' rap in front of a couple of the other parents, and Scotty acquiesced, with a twinkle in his eye, that "he may have held Brian a little longer than he needed to because you are such a good host family and important to the program's success." He then released me shortly after her challenging him, in late May.

While attending this long and arduous fifth phase, every Friday was torture for me. I was sure I was going to finally graduate, right? This was the night! Instead, I kept being severely disappointed and became very confused.

I hadn't put it together like my mom eventually did. It didn't even cross my mind. I couldn't understand what I had done wrong. I lived in dread each week that one of the Cassidys was going to come in during afterschool rap and challenge me on my past drug stories.

Had they found out that I had greatly embellished every single one? Had they found out that I was being honest when I first came here about my drug use? I was completely puzzled and lived in constant doubt and fear that spring. I didn't want to start this all over.

Chapter 33
Surprising gift
March 1993

I'm not sure I would have made it all the way through that spring if not for one night at home in early March when my parents pulled me aside to talk in private. They said that they had been discussing with each other how very proud they were of me, and they knew that, any day now, I would graduate. They had thought it would have happened by now and were slightly puzzled as to why, but knew it wasn't anything I, or they, had done. My parents then said an amazing thing, they were giving me my early graduation gift: an inexpensive, yet reliable, used car.

So, next week my dad took me used car shopping after school on my day off from group. I was so giddy; I wanted every car I test drove. My dad though, being savvy, went through several car lots before deciding on a very used and inexpensive Mazda 626. It had a stick shift, a sunroof, and was very fun to drive. It ended up being a good car until I totaled it my freshman year of college. I wouldn't be able to drive the car unless my parents were present, which meant usually on Sundays to and from church and on my days off. But I had a car and, later that month, a license, yea!

Chapter 34
Graduation!
End of May 1993

The rest of my junior year came and went in such a doldrum that I can barely remember it. I kept my head down at school, studied as hard as I could, and would get called on maybe once a week in group to talk during rap. It was just so staff could check in on me and make sure everything was ok. Usually, the only times I had to share one of my embellished druggie stories was on Friday nights. Even then, as a 5th phaser, I wasn't expected to be too in touch with my feelings while sharing. A simple glisten in the eye while telling a sad story would always work.

That late May, eighteen months after intake, I graduated Second Chance. Reverend Cassidy finally beamed out my name during promotions that Friday afternoon. I was a shell of who I was before I had entered drug treatment. I barely had a personality at all. They had melted, shaped, and recast me into another one of their statistical successes. Yea for me. Thank you so much Cassidys for playing the role of God and deciding my fate while taking away my freedom. How very Christian of you.

There was nearly a dry eye that Friday night when I blurted out on the microphone that I had graduated and ran over to the pews to hug my parents. I was so happy that I think I made the entire place vibrate with joy. That's how it felt to me at least. Almost everyone there knew I had been on fifth phase forever. I was proof that people did eventually escape from this place.

On the ride home with my parents after Friday night, no one else with us because I had graduated, my dad let me know that there was a Saturday pancake breakfast at his local Masonic lodge in Collierville. He said I could drive to meet them there in the morning if I wanted. We got home that night and removed the alarms from my bedroom windows and door. I also threw away the pee jug. Sayonara.

That next morning, I drove, all by myself, to the Masonic lodge on the Collierville Town Square. I finally felt mostly free again. It was definitely one of the best pancake breakfasts I've ever had.

Chapter 35
Aftercare
Summer 1993

One would think that because I had finally graduated from Second Chance that I had escaped that place. I knew better. I hadn't quite escaped. I still had a six-month Aftercare phase to make it through. I could still be brought back into Second Chance and put back on 1st phase. I'd seen it happen to other programmers several times over the past eighteen months. I tried my hardest during this time not to make any mistakes.

I finished my junior year at Germantown High School and ventured into my summer break with not a lot of rules, just a lot of oversight and paranoia. My Aftercare rules included: no hanging out with past druggie friends (again, <u>any</u> friend or acquaintance from my past), no relationships, no hanging out with members of the opposite sex unless in odd numbers, mandatory attendance to Friday night raps, mandatory attendance to once-a-week aftercare small group rap, no negative music (that included anything mainstream on the radio, unless it was Christian or classical radio), no R-rated movies, mandatory attendance to church on Sundays with my parents, and I was required to attend at least two Alcoholics Anonymous or Narcotics Anonymous (my choice) meetings in the Memphis metropolitan area every week.

My Aftercare group was small, only seven of us when I started. All we did was go to Alcoholics Anonymous meetings most nights and then hang out drinking coffee in the parking lot. Sometimes we'd go to a local coffee shop.

We all had our favorite A.A. and N.A. meetings that we would attend. They were our only safe hang out spots. Safe being that we knew we were pretty safe from breaking the rules there. Although, as you will read in a moment, rule breaking and serious consequences can happen in a parking lot after an A.A. meeting. However, I luckily missed it because I got put out of action for the remainder of my Aftercare.

Chapter 36
Chickenpox
July 1993

My second month into Aftercare, a bunch of Second Chance graduates and their "straight" (meaning sober) friends threw a day party one weekend. This really just included graduated programmers and their siblings that were in "good standing" with Second Chance. We all got together, about twenty to thirty of us, at one of the graduate's parents' houses and celebrated by playing volleyball and drinking non-alcoholic beverages. I remember the other programmer that I was riding with on the way home getting pulled over for speeding and receiving a ticket. Luckily, he was off his Aftercare and sober, so it wasn't that big of a deal.

Sometime that next week, I started getting itchy red spots and feeling feverish. Soon the red spots got itchier, bigger, and full of pus. It happened almost overnight. Within two days, I was covered from head to toe (seriously the top of my head all the way down to every toe) with chickenpox sores. I looked like a hideous monster. I felt like one too.

In hindsight it was kind of a blessing due to what happened during the next six weeks while I was at home in quarantine.

Six grueling weeks later, with scars of my chickenpox war that still inhabit my body to this day, I went back to my Second Chance Aftercare weekly small group rap. Surprisingly to me, I was the only one that showed up except Mrs. Cassidy. I sat down in one of the empty chairs in front of Mrs. Cassidy, stunned. Where was everyone? I thought I was in trouble for some reason. Maybe she thought it was my fault that I had missed Aftercare by getting the chickenpox and was being demoted back to fifth phase?

Instead, she informed me that a few weeks back, while I was at home with the plague, all of the other programmers on Aftercare had gotten into some serious trouble. Apparently, one of the graduates still on their Aftercare had brought a pack of cigarettes to an A.A. meeting and decided it was a good idea to convince the other graduates on their Aftercare to smoke some tobacco in their car; in the A.A. parking lot right in front of all of the other attendees milling around and chatting after the meeting.

A Second Chance graduate, who was one of the first to ever graduate from Second Chance and someone I didn't know (I sniffed them out later), had reported them the next day to the Cassidys. Even worse, no one confessed during their next Aftercare rap to the Cassidys, until one of the Aftercare programmers eventually caved. She also spilled that they were listening to rock music as well and that this wasn't the first time. To make matters worse, there were six of them, three males and three females. That meant that they were also not following the "no pairs" rule.

The Cassidys were not happy and sent all of them back to third phase. Seriously, every single one of them. I guess Second Chance now had a good influx of oldcomers to host newcomers again.

I was floored, so grateful I wasn't with the Aftercare group at that A.A. meeting and also left wondering what that meant for me. Mrs. Cassidy then said the unthinkable. Since no one was left in my Aftercare group, I didn't have to finish the remaining three months. Congratulations, I was done!

I would like to say I felt tremendous relief, but I still felt like it was some kind of trap or set-up. I continued playing the good church boy for several months, if not several years, after that. The main reason was that I was terrified everyone was watching me and the slightest screw up would send me back to Second Chance. I don't think that terror ever truly went away. It certainly played a large part in my eventual OCD diagnosis.

Chapter 37
Senior fall at Germantown High
Fall 1993

Since my senior year of high school was only a couple of weeks away, and I was still going to Friday night raps (even while off my Aftercare, fearful of being sent back to Second Chance), I decided to remain at Germantown High School that fall. I had zero friends to hang out with or talk to, but I could at least now talk to girls one-on-one at school. I met a very cool, platonic friend in one of my classes that way. She loved to call me Rainbow Bright on account of the star-shaped chickenpox scar permanently imprinted into my right cheek. I am a big blusher, with bright red cheeks, so I'm sure it made my star shine whenever she called me that. Although brief, our friendship did brightly shine. She helped me snap back to reality in a gentle and loving way.

I skated a very fine line that fall term. With my parents' support, I slowly integrated my way back into the Collierville Methodist Church while still going to A.A. meetings and appeasing Second Chance. I wouldn't be eighteen for another year, so I wasn't going to fuck it up if I could help it.

My nightly nightmares were filled with me being sent back to first phase at Second Chance. I would wake up drowning in sweat, terrified that I was still in Second Chance. I remember my mind taking its time to slowly re-awaken out of its slumber. It started slowly, but gently, in almost imperceivable ways.

For instance, I changed the wording of the morning song that was permanently stuck in my head, "It's time to wake up, time to wake up, time to wake up and go to drug rehab," by replacing the words "drug rehab" with "school." I would sing it out loud to myself and correct it to "school" if I said it wrong. It worked. Eventually that song faded out of my daily routine.

I also started going back to Taekwondo classes that fall. Since I had been away for so long, the instructor had stripped me of my black belt rank and demoted me down one rank to red belt. It was fair, since I'd only had the black belt for a little while before I went into Second Chance. I spent the next nine months in training and proudly regained my black belt. I started teaching Taekwondo for several years after that.

However, going back to Collierville Methodist Church and trying to integrate myself back into any type of social situation was tricky. One Sunday evening, I ended up getting the courage to show up to my old church out-of-the-blue. Since I now had the freedom to drive and a car, my old Methodist Youth Fellowship (MYF) group was only five minutes away from my house. I had a lot of childhood friends who had nothing to do with drugs and alcohol that hung out there, or at least had. Unfortunately, they were older now and didn't attend MYF that much. I did see Mr. Ed and a few childhood friends that I hadn't seen in forever. It was an emotional night.

I started making MYF and Wednesday night Bible study regularly towards the end of fall while connecting with more past friends. Most of them were very accepting and happy to see me again. However, not all of my old church friends were happy that I was back.

One night, a couple of MYF meetings later, one of my past best friends, Scott, met me in the parking lot with a very cold and distant stare. I hadn't seen Scott in over two years, and he immediately let me know that he was very mad at me for getting busted and going to drug treatment. He said that his parents came down on him really hard after I left because they were convinced that I had been a negative influence on his life, and he thought I had lied to him about my drug and alcohol use while we were friends, which I hadn't. Oh, the irony. I thought he was going to try and fight me.

Other close church friends would reveal that too, with one saying he was grounded for a whole month when I got in trouble; he hadn't done a thing wrong. None of them knew what exactly had happened to me or how I ended up in Second Chance in the first place. To them, I just disappeared one day and abandoned them.

However uncomfortable it was, going back and seeing old friends was Heaven to me. I was giddy and grateful. Shortly later, I started hanging out with those friends after school and on some of the weekends. We'd mainly play basketball. It was definitely what I needed at that time.

By the beginning of December of 1993, my Collierville church friends had convinced me to go back to Collierville High for the last semester of my senior year.

Anybody I had ever done drugs with was older than me and had already graduated, so it made sense to me as well. I was optimistically enthusiastic and prayed for the best. I took a leap forward and applied for a transfer back to Collierville High School, home of the Dragons.

Chapter 38

Christmas 1993

By the time Christmas of 1993 came around, my parents and I had been able to successfully disassociate ourselves from Second Chance and weren't attending any of Second Chance's, or Central Church's, functions. I think my parents had begun to realize that I wasn't going to go crazy and become the drug fiend Second Chance said I would become without strict discipline. They realized that, instead, what happened was the complete opposite.

Something had been stolen from me. It was hard for me to really laugh and be me. I had lost who I was by stifling my inner self and cramming it into a cave for two years. My parents had paid $10,000 and devoted two years of their lives for this outcome. The salt in the wound being that, technically, I was another success in Second Chance's "eyes."

I would later learn through therapy that this was when a lot of my OCD began happening for the first time. I started to continuously perform rituals in my head and assign random circumstances to possible facts. I would try to connect everything together so I could avoid something worse. If I had a bad day at school, it was because of something that I did out of order, such as not rinsing my hair the right number of times in the shower.

I would also apply this insane logic to things happening in real-time. For example, if I heard a song on the radio when I arrived at home and my parents were angry at me, I would associate that song with my parents being mad. So, I'd turn it off and back on whenever it came on, making sure to hear it a second time to balance it out.

I would then start to perform the ritual in an opposite way as well. If a song came on and my parents were in a good mood, I would associate that song with that good outcome. If I didn't repeat it the same way, then the good outcome would turn bad.

I also started doing a lot of other weird things privately. If I noticed myself stepping in front of a mirror, I would step out of the mirror frame, and then step back in. If I saw the minutes on a digital clock shift and the numbers didn't add up to a number I liked, then I would stare at the clock after sixty seconds had passed in order to see a new number. I had to actually watch the minute change. If I touched something that felt "off" to me (like the edge of a table), then I would touch it again to balance the feeling out.

At one point in my life, I had built up and assigned meaning to over one hundred rituals. Easily performing up to fifty rituals a day. I would also assign numbers in the mix to represent off and on, a binary system. I was trying to connect and balance everything.

It was madness, and it was also exhausting. But, for some reason, it would put my mind and body at ease for a little while after I completed a ritual. It was like a short and immediate dose of comfort and relief. I wouldn't be diagnosed and receive help for that mental health gift resulting from Second Chance until my late thirties.

It would be several years before I would be brave enough to try alcohol again. At the age of twenty years, shortly after my fifthyear of sobriety, I had a few drinks with a friend. I had a great time. I didn't turn into a monster. The mental disorders I got thanks to my Second Chance experience are the real monsters.

One of my all-time favorite movies is the 1957 film called "The Bridge on the River Kwai." At the very end of the movie, one of the characters loudly exclaims when everything goes to shit, "Madness! Madness ...

madness!" I think of that quote a lot when I reflect on my Second Chance experience. I'm a big, strong man; but even today that pain can sometimes quickly bring me to my knees.

Part 3

A Gentle Ripple of Love

Chapter 39
New Year 1994

This is where my story gently gets a little brighter. By the end I hope my ascent out of madness is clearly seen. However, it will take me a while to get there, a long journey with a lot of experimentation and many twists and turns.

I continued to go to church and A.A. meetings over the winter break of my senior year of high school. Most of my friends though, other than the few left at church, were older and had vamoosed from Collierville as quickly as they could. So, I ended up meeting and making a lot of teenage and young adult friends at the Alcoholics Anonymous meetings. Some were graduates from Second Chance, some from other treatment centers, and a few had gotten there by really having a problem.

Most of us though were older teenagers scared out of our wits and believed that, if we went anywhere near drugs and alcohol, our lives would fall completely apart. So, we supported each other and started hanging out and doing sober things; like going to a restaurant for coffee after Alcoholics Anonymous meetings. I finally felt like I had a semi-social life again.

By the time the New Year had come and gone, I felt I was ready to go back to Collierville High School for the final portion of my senior year.

Chapter 40
Back to Collierville High

My first day back to my old high school was, to say the least, a little nerve racking. The senior graduating class at Collierville High at the time was around 200 students, with no more than 1,000 or so total students at the school. So, not a large school, but not a tiny one either. I wasn't sure what to expect. Was everyone going to gawk at me and talk behind my back while I walked down the halls?

In hindsight, most everybody was pretty cool about my return. Both the teachers and the students that knew me welcomed me back with open arms. I got to reconnect with some old friends during lunches and share a little bit about what had happened to me. It was almost like the past two years didn't happen, almost.

The one very glaring difference being that I hadn't integrated into any social circles at school. Everyone I knew seemed like they had grown up and had some sort of purpose, even if it was just short-term. They knew where they fit in the hierarchy of things. I, having missed out on the past two years of social experiences, was in the complete dark. I didn't go to, or get invited to, any senior afterschool parties. The other students had no clue what to make of me, I was completely different from my old self. I didn't belong.

One of the teachers didn't like that I was back either. One of the mornings that first week, while I was walking down the hallway, a teacher I barely remembered walked out of her classroom, turned towards me, and stopped in her tracks with a look of utmost horror on her face. That look was directed towards me.

After a short pause, she got the courage to march up to me and said in a very angry, and frightened, tone, "what are you doing back in school?" I told her that "I had just transferred back in and…"

She didn't let me finish. Instead, she went completely nuts, while turning around and walking down the hall to the principal's office; all the while yelling that she couldn't believe they would let me back into this school. I slowly followed her to the principal's office and sat outside in the reception area, waiting for the principal to come get me and explain what the heck was going on with that teacher. What had I done wrong?

After several minutes of waiting, the teacher came back out of the office, strolled up to me, and apologized. For what, I didn't know at the time. She then turned and walked out the door.

The principal came out of his office, saw me waiting, and told me to come on into his office. He was familiar with what I had been through, I had met with him on the first day back to school, and he seemed very apologetic.

Come to find out, the teacher that went into the principal's office was ranting and raving to the principal that she couldn't believe they would let me back into school. She had gotten me confused with my older brother and really thought I was him. I, still to this day, don't know what my brother ever did to her. I'm sure it was something bad, so I am glad we got it semi-sorted out.

About a month into one of my classes, I realized that I was very alone at school. It happened while we were all milling around and chatting while the teacher was out of the classroom. I had finally gotten some of my silliness back that had been robbed of me and was slowly starting to learn how to express it in a social setting again.

Scott, my previous friend through our church MYF group, was in that class. He had changed, a lot. He now liked country music, wore big belt buckles, and hung out with the more rural cowboy boot crowd, which was one of the most popular social circles at Collierville at the time, the others being athletics and band. I thought we were cool and that his anger towards me had dissipated, it hadn't.

Standing around with Scott and six other kids in my class, I made some kind of silly joke. I'm sure my physical demeanor matched my joke. Scott, like so many others in my past, didn't appreciate my silliness. He turned around, grabbed me by the front of my shirt collar, and walked me backwards, pinning me against a metal cabinet locker. I was stunned and didn't fight back. He wasn't hurting me, and, again, I was stunned.

While pinning me against the cabinet doors, he yelled "Brian, what is your fucking problem? Why are you happy right now? When are you going to ever grow up?" with a few other choice words mixed in. I guess we weren't cool. He let me go, and I walked away, never talking to Scott again after that. We had obviously grown worlds apart.

It was a good lesson for me. It reminded me that people in the "normal world" had different rules and conventions that I needed to adhere to. It just took me that spring, and the rest of my life, to readjust. I went through a lot of awkward moments at school during that time where I thought I was being funny, but no one laughed.

I also couldn't get a date to save my life. I don't blame the ladies. I was a tall, gangly mess of a boy wearing semi-dress clothes who had been through a long period of drug treatment. I reeked of desperation and inexperience. I wasn't a "bad boy," I was a "no way boy."

I did meet one girl who eventually became a very good friend; it was by accident. Shortly into my last semester of high school, I saw her sitting by herself in my health class. For some reason, every "cowboy/cowgirl" at Collierville High was in that health class. They were a very popular clique. The teacher taught us how to square dance that semester. Scott was there as well. The pride of the class.

So, being that it was health and that I had plenty of free social time during class, I was relinquished to being on the outside trying to fit in. I would try and laugh at their jokes, but it was exhausting, and I was getting nowhere. I definitely didn't fit in.

It was during one of those times when I turned around and saw one of the most unique and beautiful young woman that I'd ever seen. She was alone, almost invisible, reading a Morrissey book by herself. It was 1994, she had very short hair, and she was bitching. Unfortunately, I soon found out that she had an older boyfriend for the past two years. She had transferred into Collierville High a year ago.

I slowly approached her like I would a deer in the wild and said, in the meekest voice I could muster, "Hi, I'm Brian, whatcha reading?" She said, "not much, just Morrissey," and then we struck it off. By the end of the class, I found out that one of her best friends was really good friends with a guy that also went to Second Chance. I knew him, he was one of my newcomers at one point and had graduated from Second Chance a few months ago. It was a small world.

She also had some really cool and rich friends in Germantown and invited me to hang after school. I happily hung out with them at one of their parents' mansions. Since all of them knew what Second Chance was, they were really cool and understanding of me. One of my first cool experiences with a sweet group of kids.

They would usually smoke marijuana, but I always abstained. They would then almost always say they didn't care and that I was cool to hang out with even if I wasn't high. I believe them. I had a shit ton of innocent and semi-legal fun times with them during that time span. However, I was still also going to Alcoholic Anonymous, and sometimes Narcotics Anonymous, meetings; still convinced that if I touched alcohol or drugs that I would turn into a monster.

Chapter 41

Senior prom

This is a very short chapter. As mentioned before, I had no game when it came to the ladies. I hadn't a shot at going to my senior prom.

A month before the prom, one girl that had also gone through Second Chance and was a few years older had taken pity and said she would go to the prom with me. However, she politely bailed a few weeks before it happened. I'm pretty sure I went to an Alcoholics Anonymous meeting on my prom night. Everyone I tell this story to says that I didn't miss much.

Chapter 42
Pink Floyd

One really awesome thing that did happen to me that spring was when I overheard a classmate say out loud that he was standing in line that following weekend to purchase tickets to the Pink Floyd concert in Nashville. He wanted to know if anyone else wanted in? I immediately said "yes" and forked over my money. Call it my primal self, begging to be unleashed.

The Pink Floyd concert at Vanderbilt Stadium in Nashville was unbelievably awesome. There were two inflatable pigs, one on each side of the stage, several stories tall! They also had a huge disco ball that came out during "Shine on You Crazy Diamond," and a choreographed film on a large projection screen above the stage during the entire show.

My seats were on the lawn, right in the middle. The huge disco ball came out of a giant box that was right beside me. It was fantastic, even though I was completely sober. One of the best shows to this date that I've ever seen.

Chapter 43
High-school graduation
June 1994

Well, June came around, and I'd made it. I had finally finished high school. My senior class did the normal graduation ceremony thing at a convention center in Memphis with a chaperoned party at the Collierville community center afterwards. I didn't get invited to an afterparty and was home by eleven.

I was still seventeen, so I couldn't get into much fun, especially with Second Chance looming like a Damocles sword hovering over my neck. I mainly just hung out with one friend and walked home with her. I was good friends at the time with her older boyfriend. Not much of a celebration, but at least I had college and a summer break to look forward to. I tried putting Second Chance in the rearview mirror as best as I could.

Chapter 44
Summer before college
1994

After graduating from high school, my parents were very supportive of me going to college. I agreed that it was a good choice at the time. So, that summer after high school my time was spent working at a NAPA auto parts warehouse in Memphis in order to save for college, attending Alcoholics Anonymous and Narcotics Anonymous meetings with my "straight/sober" group of friends, and hanging out with my "cool" friends in Germantown. I still remained completely straight and sober. I lived with non-stop dread and fear that I was going to mess up and be sent back to Second Chance until I was twenty-one.

It was a mixed summer. I had to work nights at a NAPA warehouse, so I really didn't have a lot of free time to socialize. I did slice my hand open one night with a box-cutter at NAPA, which introduced to me the importance of worker safety, so that sucked. However, on the bright side, my rich friends' parents in Germantown all had awesome swimming pools, and I got to socialize with them whenever I could.

I also had a huge crush on one of my friends who lived in one of those rich houses in Germantown. She was the youngest of three sisters, smoking hot, and nice to boot. Unfortunately, she had a long-term boyfriend. I was also a shy virgin, so I didn't know how to approach her even if she didn't have a boyfriend.

Then there were my "straight/sober" friends that slowly drifted away from meetings over the summer, with new "straight/sober" friends arriving to meetings every week. It was all a difficult balance for me to maintain, but I did it somehow and had fun whenever I could.

Chapter 45

Mississippi State University (Honor's College)

Fall 1994

Since I graduated from high school with a high grade point average and also scored really well on my college entrance exams, I had several choices of top regional colleges that I could attend. I ended up picking what I thought was the best offer at the time: a full ride with room and board to Mississippi State University. In hindsight, due to my lack of social maturity, I should have stayed around Memphis where my support was greater and attended Rhodes College instead. But Rhodes College wasn't going to pay me to go there, and, since their tuition was fairly exorbitant, I settled on the most cost-effective choice I had. I took a chance on Mississippi State's new on-campus extension called their "Honor's College." I was starting a clean slate in Starkville, Mississippi.

Us freshmen that were in the "Honor's College" got to stay in our very own co-ed dorm building that was on the large, sprawling campus that took up most of Starkville, Mississippi. Unfortunately, Mississippi State University's version of co-ed was that the females lived on one side of the building (in its multi-story wing) and the males lived on the other side (in their own multi-story wing). No one was allowed on the other side. The only thing co-ed about it was that we shared a central lobby and recreation room where we'd watch movies together.

The rooms were typical, small dorm rooms with a metal twin bunk bed and two desks in each one. I have fond memories of being on my bunk bed at night and feeling the rough concrete masonry blocks with my fingers while envisioning that I was in prison. Dorm rooms are weird.

I met my roommate my first day there, and he was weird as well. He was the cool kind of weird. He hailed from Louisiana, played guitar, and was fun to be around.

The only real gripe I ever had with him was that he was short. No, I'm not shaming him because of his height. It's because one day he hung a metal stop sign in the middle of our room at around 6'2" off the ground without thinking about warning me. That same day, me tiredly walking into my dorm room after classes resulted in my dumb ass nicking my forehead really good on that sign. The stop sign did its job. One of the many things I've nicked my forehead on throughout my life.

Starkville, Mississippi was a very small town at that time. The majority of the population was comprised of the Mississippi State University campus and its staff. So, there was very little us bored college students could do for fun except drink alcohol and party.

Most Mississippi State fraternities and sororities had to be discreet though, especially since there was a strict no drinking alcohol on campus rule as well. You were also in much more trouble if you got caught drinking alcohol on campus while underage. A few of the fraternities, one in particular that I became well acquainted with, decided to have their houses off campus in order to get around that troublesome rule.

Now, since I was still sober, I immediately got delegated as the designated driver whenever me and my freshman friends (one of our dorm mates was pledging) would go to the parties. I liked going to the parties, they were still fun even if I wasn't drinking. I quickly made more friends at the fraternity parties and, even though I decided rushing and joining a fraternity was not for me, I was enjoying myself those first few months at MSU.

I would occasionally go to the one Alcoholics Anonymous meeting space in Starkville for meetings when not in class. There weren't any kids my age at them though. I didn't really have any support, but I was determined that I wasn't going to drink or get high. I just kind of stayed sober out of shear will. I was still afraid of becoming a monster like Second Chance said I would become if I had one drop of booze.

Chapter 47
The freshman incident
Fall 1994

One night, late into the fall of my first year of college, I decided to go to a party at one of the off-campus fraternities. I was the designated driver, still sober, but had fun at the party anyway. I left the frat house around 1:00 am in my car with four dorm mates, three in the backseat and one up front. All four of them piss ass drunk and having the time of their lives.

On the way through the center of Starkville, there was a stretch of road that had a speed limit of 20 mph. The police meant it too. If you went over 20 mph, there was a really good chance you were getting pulled over; especially late at night. So, while doing the smart thing and going the speed limit, a pair of headlights came speeding up behind us and got right on my ass. Then the vehicle started flashing its brights.

It looked like a jeep in my rearview mirror and not a cop. I was just about to use my turn signal and pull over so I could let this mad person pass, when my very drunk dorm mate in the front seat, whom I barely knew, decided to lean out of the passenger side window of my car and flip the vehicle behind us off. Then the other three morons in my backseat decided to join in. One of the morons even tried to moon them through my backseat window, bless his heart.

As you can guess that didn't go over well with the jeep. It accelerated and pulled up beside us in the oncoming lane (there was zero traffic). Two older teenagers were sitting in the front seat. I wasn't exactly sure what they were screaming at me, but I knew they didn't want a hug. The jeep then slowed down, got behind me, and stayed right on my ass. Shortly after, I pulled onto campus and, expecting them to drive off, they followed us all the way to our dorm parking lot instead. I was scared. My passengers were drunk and wanted to fight.

When we stepped out of the car in the well-lit parking lot, the jeep parked about thirty feet behind us. Two large teenagers came bolting out of the jeep. One of them reached into the back of it and pulled out a baseball bat. They both came walking toward us with the intent to do us much harm.

I, again being the only sober one in my party, tried to step in-between and apologized on my friends' behalf. A few of my friends though blurted out around the same time that the teens could go fornicate themselves in many different ways. That only seemed to enrage the teens more.

They came to within ten feet of us and stopped, realizing that there were only two of them and five of us. The one with the baseball bat seemed intent that they could win though. As he stepped forward, a bright light shone upon him and a campus police car flashed its lights as it pulled up. He froze.

Two campus police officers came running out of the car and demanded to know what was going on. I tried my best to explain the situation and was completely honest with them. We all five had campus identification and lived in the dorm that was next to the parking lot.

The two teenagers in the jeep did not have campus identification, they apparently were seniors at the local high school. The one that was driving did not have a driver's license, but the other one did and was seventeen. Even though we all explained to the campus police that the teens had followed us on campus, the police just took the bat away from the kids in the jeep and told them not to come back. They made the kid with the license drive.

I don't know exactly why, but that experience really shook me at the time. I became extremely nervous and concerned that those kids were going to come back and vandalize my car while I wasn't there. It was all I could think of for the next week. I finally ended up parking my car in another parking lot and walking a long way to my dorm for the rest of the semester just to get some peace of mind.

Chapter 48
Headed home
Winter 1994/95

Gray would be the best color to describe how I was feeling by the end of my freshman semester. It wasn't Mississippi State University's fault, I would have felt the same way at any college away from home. I was homesick and the college life wasn't really jelling with my sobriety. I was too scared to let loose, and life seemed to march forward while I had to observe it through a hazy rain-streaked windowpane. Watching the water drops flowing down on the other side of the glass but never being able to actually touch and feel them.

Come Thanksgiving, I was severely depressed and had decided that I was going to hang up my hat and come back home where my support was at the time. So, I applied for a transfer to the local Memphis college, The University of Memphis, and my parents graciously let me back into their house after the fall semester ended. I gave up my scholarship at Mississippi State University and had to take out a co-loan with my parents to go to school from then on out. Neither the University of Memphis, nor any other college, was willing to honor their previous scholarship offers now that I had attended a semester somewhere else. Seemed unfair to me at the time, but, hey, that's life.

I was able to get back to my friends that were on the sobriety circuit. Coffee, cigarettes, A.A. meetings, and N. A. meetings became my winter and beyond. I didn't realize then that sometimes it's best to move on from things because they eventually fade away. That's what started happening to my sober young adult friends.

Through that Christmas break, a lot of my friends "relapsed." Every week I'd hear of another friend who had used and was now hanging out with other relapsed friends. My friends were dropping fast, and I had no idea how they were doing once they dropped out of the sobriety circuit. It slowly sapped any life I had left out of me. I didn't understand the ramifications of time like I do now.

Like a punch to my sternum, life delivered yet another layer to add to my onion of despair. Right after New Year's 1995, and before I was to attend college at the University of Memphis that spring, I was t-boned by a pick-up truck in an intersection near the college in Memphis. It totaled my car but luckily no one was seriously injured. One of my best friends was the only passenger, and he wasn't wearing a seatbelt. He was 6'6" and his forehead made a bubble impression on my windshield. He laughed and shook it off afterwards. Damn it if he wasn't tough. I had my seatbelt on.

I quickly got the cheapest car I could find through a friend's stepdad later that week. The car broke down the next day (the transmission stopped working) and my friend's stepdad refused to take it back. My dad, God bless him, came to my rescue and gave me a small loan for another cheap car. I was able to get, for less than $1,000, a canary yellow 1978 Lincoln Continental 4-door with pop-up headlights. It was the deluxe edition, with a wood-grained dashboard trim, leather seats and all, and had been sitting in a widow's garage for the past ten years. I answered her ad in the local newspaper.

Lucky me for sure. That car was in perfect condition and drove like a dream. I could also fit eight people in it comfortably. I fell in love with it. I didn't fall in love with the gas mileage though, but it was still worth it. It rode like a cloud.

Chapter 49
Getting to see Jerry
Spring 1995

Still clinging to sobriety ideals and the sober way of life, I trodded along at the University of Memphis, driving back and forth from my parents' home in Collierville every day for classes and then again at night for A.A./N.A. meetings. I also bounced between small and mundane part-time jobs.

By February I had made enough money to, with my parents' help, be able to rent a small house in a poor area in Memphis with a sober roommate. My dad promised to help me with the bills when I struggled if I kept up my good grades at the University of Memphis. He kept his word, God bless him.

By the end of March 1995, I was ecstatic. Several months prior, I had wisely stood in line and bought tickets to the 1995 April Fool's Grateful Dead concert that was coming to Memphis. Nobody was sure that it was real, even though we had stood in line at Ticketmaster and bought real tickets. The Grateful Dead stopped coming to Memphis in the early 1970s with good reason. They were not welcomed by most of the Mid-South, and they knew it. To be performing a two-day set on April Fools and the next day did not seem real to anyone. It had to be a hoax, right?

Nope. Sure enough, the Grateful Dead performed both nights. I saw them the first night, one of the last shows that Jerry Garcia, their lead singer/guitarist, was still alive for. I remember that he played and sung fairly well that night. He definitely gave the audience some memorable energy. We danced our assess off.

One of my friends and I camped out after the show in my car in a parking lot near Shakedown Street, the nightly market after shows. Picture a very large Farmer's Market late at night with nothing but hippies, music, and arts and crafts and other wares being peddled so those hippies could make it to the next show.

Interesting fact. Did you know that the Grateful Dead supported self-help meetings during their shows? They were targeted towards A.A., N.A., and other folk needing substance abuse or mental health support. The meetings took place during intermissions. They announced it to everyone during the show and provided a safe space at the show for the meetings. This surprised the heck out of me. I thought I was the only sober one there.

It wasn't until later that I had the wisdom to see that alcohol and drugs weren't needed to "get" the Grateful Dead and a lot of fans don't partake. You don't have to be stoned to get their music, man. However, objectively looking back on it, I do wish I had been stoned. I believe it would have enhanced the experience even more for me. I also believe it would have helped me cope better with the crushing depression that was starting to swallow me whole.

I remember going to a psychiatrist around that time, and they prescribed me a drug. One of the first class of anti-depressants. It turned me into one of those steroid jocks I used to see on after school television shows. I felt and acted like a steroid monster and very quickly got off them. I was convinced coffee and nicotine were the only drugs I needed. I was wrong.

Chapter 50
AP Psychology
Summer 1995

After a semester under my belt, I was still able to get into the University of Memphis's Honor's Psychology tract with supplemental pre-med courses. I was contemplating being a psychiatrist at the time, determined I could change the profession for the good. I made good grades while maintaining a full course load. My favorite course was AP Biopsychology, and I signed up to run some lab trials on some brave students who also wanted extra credit over the summer. I videotaped finger trial mazes that related to laterality of the brain.

Due to this course, I got to know the professor well. I also learned a new word, "grants." Everything in the biopsychology field depended on grants, and a lot of grants don't leave much money for the researcher/professor. It was a risky business to undertake. Praying each year to the "grant giver" gods.

She did not make a lot of money, lived in a very small house, and drove a very old car. That certainly played into my slow withdrawal from college and my fade from the "sober" way of thinking. I wasn't sure if this career route was really the one I wanted.

Chapter 51
Four years of sobriety
Fall 1995 – Fall 1996

I continued to stay sober throughout my sophomore year of college and trodded along through a full course load at the University of Memphis. I was also finally able to land a job I could stand at a local bank check sorting facility. The only problem was that to increase my hours, I had to take the graveyard shift. It was hard working six to eight hours at night, going to morning and early afternoon classes, sleeping, waking, and then going to work at midnight again.

It was hard to get any sleep, especially if the sun was out. Black-out curtains and eventually cutting cardboard, wrapping aluminum foil around it, and shoving it in the window helped. But I still knew the sun was out there every time I'd lay down, just beckoning me to join it.

This routine got old, real quick, but I was able to maintain it for a year or so while keeping my grades up. I was still feeling awful inside though. It felt like I had a gaping empty hole in the center of my chest that nothing could fill. It hurt, like deep hunger pains.

I tried to fill that hole with God, Jesus Christ, martial arts, and A.A./N.A. meetings, but, after my experience with Second Chance, I was having a very hard time connecting with my spiritual side, even less so religion. My mind, body, and soul were torn. Nothing was right for me. For the first time, I started seriously contemplating suicide.

That October, I celebrated my fourth year of sobriety with my few remaining sober friends and some new sober friends I had made. It was very dull. That next year was also very dull and unmemorable for me.

I was still in a gray haze of depression and spiraling. I just couldn't feel good, no matter what I did. Therefore, my memories of the entire year exist beyond a veil that I can't penetrate or describe.

My grades started slipping as well. I started settling for "B's" instead of "A's." I had become disillusioned on the science behind a lot of the psychology I was learning. A lot of it was just theories and bullshit. It reminded me more and more of Second Chance.

I remember snippets, but for the most part, I've blanked that entire year out of my mind. Even most of the stuff I learned in school. I would soak it up, regurgitate it for my professors, and then go back to my life of sadness and OCD rituals. My OCD rituals were the only thing that brought any real happiness to me then. That happiness was fleeting though and would only last for a short moment. I would then make up the next OCD ritual to occupy my time with and temporarily make myself happy.

I was also a very angry young man that entire year. It's a miracle that I didn't physically hurt myself or others during that time. I was a freakin' mess.

Chapter 52
Five years of sobriety
October 1996

I made it to five years of sobriety that October at the age of twenty. Problem was, hardly any of my other friends had. I was the rare, sober unicorn, I guess. Making it harder on myself, I still interacted with some of those young friends that had "relapsed." Miraculously, they hadn't turned into the monsters that Second Chance and other treatment centers said they would. They seemed to be having a good time instead.

Unfortunately, there were some that sadly had too good of a time and ended up departing from this world way too early. I knew those kids well and cared for them deeply. We hurt the same. My thought on the whole thing is that it wasn't drugs and alcohol that did them in, it was us, society, and our stupid, illogical rules. Luckily for me, I had developed a "no needle" policy during my drug exploration phase. There was no way that my OCD was going to let me stick a needle in my veins.

Those young adults who didn't develop that philosophy, my friends, would have hurt themselves any way they could to escape the hurt that had been imposed upon them as children. They would have gone to any lengths to be happy just for one moment, to escape their worst enemy, themselves. I know that is irony; it's also madness. Instead of us caring for them like a community should have, we shut them away and labeled them "alcoholics, addicts, and degenerates." We allowed their circle of hurt to continue. We fed their hurt and fueled their hate.

We still do the same today. We continue to buy into fear. We label them and then shun them. They're just kids for God's sake. Those kids needed love. Real love. Warm, caring love. Not tough, cold love. We, as a society, continue to fail those like them on a daily basis. Their cold bodies are constantly on my mind.

Even in sobriety and with "working the program," I wasn't feeling the love at that moment of time. Several days after my five-year sobriety anniversary, I went to my last A.A. meeting. That next night I decided to go buy a drink from the local grocery store and bring it back home. I went with one of my close friends who was twenty-one and could buy the alcohol. He had fallen off the bandwagon several months prior. Almost everyone had by that time.

I did it upright too, in spectacular fashion. I got myself a 40 oz. bottle of Hurricane malt liquor. We called it "Slurricane" back in the day. We went back to my place, and I got blitzed. I hadn't laughed that hard in a long, long time.

I remember sitting in my chair, giggling, and doing that weird thing amateur drunks always seem to do – blowing on the top of the 40 oz. bottle to make train whistle noises. The last time I remember feeling that silly and free of my internal shackles was when I had gotten sloshed on boxed wine right before Second Chance. It was exhilarating. It was freeing.

I ventured over to a friend's apartment that week after they found out I had relapsed. They held a special party for me with a large number of my other relapsed friends that I hadn't seen in a long, long time. They had a 5' long (yes, that's five foot long) red, plastic bong loaded and ready for me. It was a two-person bong, one to light it and one to inhale the smoke on the other end. I got the green hit (first flame on the marijuana flower bowl).

I coughed my ass off. Everyone laughed and started passing the bong around. As it was going around, and my coughing subsided, a warm, internal, tingling sensation came out of nowhere, springing from my heart. As that warm sensation slowly spread all over my body, I started giggling and couldn't stop. That turned the whole apartment into giggle-monsters. Us giggly, silly monsters. Shame on us for taking a moment out of this mad life to feel good.

Chapter 53
Discovering Oregon
December 1996

I finished the fall of my junior year of college a lot happier then when I started it. I hadn't turned into a monster. Sure, I was experimenting and hadn't learned why balance and discipline are truly important, but I had to learn somehow, someday. All long-term treatment had done was lock me away from reality and not show me how to sanely deal with it. I was already broken, and treatment couldn't fix me. In my opinion at the time, treatment's cure was an alternative almost worse than death.

I reconnected with a lot of friends over the first couple of months of my relapse. At the beginning of December, one of those friends headed to Portland, Oregon with his girlfriend. They invited me to fly out and visit them over the winter break. I bought a round-trip ticket to Portland for one week, taking off work for the vacation.

When I arrived at the Portland airport, my friend took me back to his apartment on the bus. On that day, I encountered a lot of beautiful scenery on the way from the airport to downtown. Oregon was lush, green, and beautiful. What captivated me the most though was the freeing feeling I felt. It just seemed to me the air was lighter in weight than it was in Memphis.

The marijuana was better for sure. Way, way better. We got really high when I got back to my friend's apartment. We continued to get really high throughout that next week. I ended up capping off the trip by having a blast at a New Year's warehouse rave (underground music party) in Portland. There were at least 2,000 other kids there in the multi-level warehouse with DJ's spread throughout. All having a blast and dancing their assess off.

Chapter 54
The mysterious illness
January 1997

As you may have guessed by now, I was a moron at that age as most young adults are. I did not know how to healthily take care of myself. I was living off Ramen noodles, soda, coffee, and nicotine. I barely drank water and took zero vitamins or supplements. It had been my routine for the past two years. Again, I was a moron and knew no better. I'm not sure I cared much at the time either.

My body knew better though, even at that young age of twenty. At the very end of my week in Portland, I suddenly became very ill. I thought I had a very bad flu, and, after becoming severely dehydrated at my friend's apartment on my last night there, I packed up my things into my suitcase and took an emergency cab ride to the hospital.

They checked me in, but they couldn't really figure out what was wrong with me. Doctors chalked it up to the flu mixed with dehydration and stuck an IV in me. After a few hours on the IV, I slowly snapped out of my fugue, my fever broke, and I felt much better. I left the hospital and took a cab to the airport to wait for my plane home.

I remember feeling ill again by the time I got home to Memphis. I went home, still feeling sick for almost two weeks while not getting much better. I just laid around my place and kept chugging sodas and eating Ramen. I couldn't go to work, so they fired me. I also had to drop out of school for the semester. I eventually caved and called my mom. Worried, she picked me up and took me to the hospital. They admitted me and did the same IV treatment as the other hospital.

After a couple of hours on the IV, I perked up again. They decided to run a bunch, I mean a bunch, of blood tests on me. This included several trips with trays of vials over the next couple of hours. They couldn't find anything wrong with me, so they released me after twenty or so hours into my mom's care. She brought me back to my parents' house, took care of me, and I slowly got healthy again over the next week. Still ignorant to just how bad I was hurting my body by living off soda and junk food.

Chapter 55
My cure
Spring 1997

I stayed fairly healthy for the next couple of months, but I still wasn't taking care of my body. I really didn't want to. I'd given up and was ready to give up on everything for good.

Early into that April, I ran into one of the most peculiar of fellas who was sleeping on a friend's couch. He was a hippie, reminded me of a Deadhead, but said he was in this thing called a Rainbow Gathering. It sounded cool at the time, but what I was most interested in was this guy. He gave off such a feminine and peaceful vibe. He was different than anyone I'd ever met, and I was instantly intrigued.

After hanging out with him over that next week, I found out many cool things about him. The most interesting one was that he knew someone who grew psilocybin mushrooms. He gave me a bunch of mushrooms as he was leaving out-of-town to continue on the Rainbow Gathering circuit. I went home that night and took a very heavy dose alone. I never saw that guy again.

I'd taken psychoactive mushrooms before (when I was fourteen and again just that last December), but I'd never taken such a huge dose. It was like a light switch flipped on inside of me, and I remembered who I was. My innocent inner child who loved me so much was on the other side of a wall that I had been building up since my abuse. That wall suddenly came down and love came flooding in.

It wasn't the most pleasant experience at first. I was alone and terrified. I wept while sitting on the side of my bed for at least an hour. I cried it all out. Every bit that I could.

Then, after every lost drop of wetness had been squeezed out of my eyes, I suddenly felt a tremendous relief. Just like that, I had reconnected and loved myself again. I didn't want to die. I wanted to live. I wanted to experience. I wanted to ride the madness and learn how to enjoy life. My inner child was suddenly there and demanding it. I felt like I was a kid again, and I loved that part of me.

I went through several hours after that of serious self-reflection. It wasn't a harsh reflection. I realized that madness had happened to me in my life, and that it was ok. My inner child that I was trying to protect was not mad at me, it was sad that we weren't connected. I was neglecting my inner self and, therefore, became my own worst enemy. Towards the end of my mushroom trip, I was hugging myself while rocking in a ball and telling myself I would never give up on living life again. I had a lot of catching up to do. I eventually drifted into a very deep and peaceful sleep.

Chapter 56
The next day
April 1997

I woke up the next morning to a feeling I hadn't felt since I was a child. I felt the joy, warmth, and radiance of the sun. It warmed my insides and filled that missing void inside of me. I wanted to get out of bed. In reflection, I had somehow turned back on my brain's dopamine factory. And man, it was beautiful. Life was beautiful.

I remember it being Sunday, and I immediately called my parents. I wanted to come over and spend the afternoon with them. "Was that ok with them?"

They said "yes," and I made the thirty-minute drive out to Collierville to my parents' house. When I arrived, I just lovingly hugged them and couldn't stop. We had a very teary and honest afternoon, and we discovered a lot of things about life. Mainly that madness afflicts everyone, and that we shouldn't use that as an excuse to quit living or loving.

I told my parents that I didn't know what I wanted to do, but I was certain at this point in time that it was not medical school. I explained I wanted to stay out of school that summer as well. They were very supportive. I felt free.

I got home that night, called some friends over to my place, and finished the mushrooms with them. We had a blast and acted like six-year-old kids at a slumber party all night. This included getting coloring books and crayons out that someone had and having an impromptu coloring book session. The horror of it all.

Chapter 57
1997 Alabama Regional Rainbow Gathering
April 1997

I was working a couple of part-time jobs, so don't think I was a total slacker. I had to pay the bills. I remember working at one of my jobs (delivering chicken wings) and having a shitty night. One of the customers pulled a gun on me and, in front of his friends who were playing a card game, emphasized that no one there ordered wings, and that I better leave before he shot me. That was pretty traumatic, and very overly dramatic by him. I was just trying to deliver hot wings, c'mon man.

When I got home, my roommates and several friends were there to cheer me up with a marijuana cigarette (a.k.a. a big ass joint). They also had some news they thought would help. They were going to a regional Rainbow Gathering in Alabama for a few days and wanted to know if I would come. I said, "fuck it," called in sick to work, and we left that next morning for Northern Alabama.

Now I had no idea what a Rainbow Gathering was at the time. It's ok if some of the readers have no idea what I'm talking about either. I just knew I was going camping in the woods with a bunch of hippies. I liked hippies. They seemed to be happy and peaceful. I wanted to be happy and peaceful. What a coincidence!

We arrived that same day and parked in a designated parking lot. We then hiked in with a stream of hippies from the parking lot into federal land where camping was free. When we arrived at the encampment, there were hundreds of hippies just spread about the woods doing their thing. Everyone seemed to be one with nature and the environment. It reminded me of wood elves just trying to live with nature and co-exist. It was amazing to see, and I was instantly intrigued.

For the next few days, I wandered around with my friends relearning how to camp and co-exist with nature. It was awesome! I felt reconnected to another part of myself I was missing, my love of nature. I was also introduced to my first large drum circle in the woods while on psychedelic mushrooms. Those not playing drums were dancing their bones off.

It was a magical time, and I wanted it to continue, but I also knew I had to get back to my menial jobs so that I could make rent and live in society. I couldn't even conceive how someone could disconnect from society completely and go from one Rainbow Gathering to the next without a job. Voluntary homelessness didn't make sense to me.

That next month, we had tons of Rainbow Gathering "kids" flutter through Memphis. The National Gathering was being held in Oregon that year, and a lot of the hippies were making their way there. The pinnacle was to happen on the 4th of July. One day, a couple of my close friends just took off. They came by my place on the way out and said they had space for me in their car. I couldn't take off like that, so I politely declined. I wanted to go so badly though.

I started talking to my parents about it, and they were actually supportive. I guess they had seen the positive effect that the hippie culture was having on me, and they wanted to support my happiness however they could. I gave notice to my jobs the next week and started to plan how I was going to do it.

I sold my Toyota Camry and bought a 1985 Volkswagen van. It was blue/gray and had a water-cooled engine. The back seat laid out into a bed. That's all I needed. I put a couple of stickers on it and then hung a mini-disco ball from the rearview mirror. I think I also put some fuzzy balls up around the window interior like Cheech's car - I had to keep it classy.

For the next few weeks, I saved my money and planned my trip. If I took it slow, staying at state campgrounds along the way, I had enough money to make it there and back, plus a little to spare. So, that mid-June, I took off in my Volkswagen by myself into the great unknown. We didn't have cell phones or GPS, so I brought with me my trusty road atlas that I had carefully plotted my route on.

Chapter 58

The Quattlebaum Family Reunion (Toad Suck, Arkansas)

Now, there was one thing in my childhood that my father insisted I went to every June that I thoroughly enjoyed. The Arkansas branch of Quattlebaums held a yearly family reunion in a campground at Toad Suck, Arkansas. The reunion always happened in June, and my dad was always the treasurer, or secretary, or some other type of organizer. He loved it, and we fully supported it. My brother even used to enjoy going with us before he took his trip to the dark side.

The Quattlebaums have been in America since Petter Quattelbaum landed in Philadelphia in 1736. The lineage has branched out across this beautiful nation since. One area that became densely populated in the late 1800s by the Quattlebaums was North Central Arkansas. They were mostly small farmers, and therefore, had lots and lots of children. Those children were all close cousins and would routinely get together for gatherings and other fun family activities. At one time hundreds or more Quattlebaums would gather monthly for family functions in Northwest Arkansas.

By the mid-to-late 1900s, small farming was dwindling, and so were the Quattlebaum numbers. As a result, sometime in the 1970s the Arkansas branch decided to have an annual gathering to be able to see relatives they hadn't seen all year. Every June, hundreds of Quattlebaums would descend down to a lovely campground on the Arkansas River called Toad Suck Park for a week of camping and summer fun. We always called it Toad Suck Ferry due to there being a famous ferry that used to cross the Arkansas River at that location. There is also a considerable sized dam.

Most of the time my dad would tow a pop-up camper that they had bought back when I was a young child. It didn't have A/C, so it was a little brutal to be in during the summer, but we made it work. I have fond memories of staying out really late, eating watermelon, and catching lightning bugs in jars with my other cousins.

I also have memories of my brother and older cousins trying to poke alligator gar with long sticks while trying not to get bitten. These fish were huge, almost five feet in length, and had a long mouth that looked eerily similar to an alligator's mouth. So did the teeth.

The gar would actually jump out of the small sandbar pools they had gotten stuck in when the river level dropped and try to bite you. Especially when you tried to poke them with a stick. I always kept a respectable distance away. My great-aunts would usually come by during this and yell at the older boys to leave them gar alone.

The Arkansas Quattlebaums were really good folk. That's where I honed my fishing skills, learned basic camping, and discovered the Arkansas family folklore behind the Quattlebaum name. I remember hearing the folk tale for the first time when I was six, sitting around the Quattlebaum campground group circle with thirty or so elder Quattlebaums, all of them taking turns sharing tales.

Quattlebaum was originally spelled "Quattelbaum". In the mid-1800s it was Americanized by a democratic vote by the Quattlebaums. Our descendants can be traced back to Germany, but there is a lot of confusion on what the name actually means. Baum means tree, but what exactly is a Quattel?

My Arkansas branch told a folktale that had been passed down over the generations. Their version was that a "Quattel" was a very slow growing bush or tree that produced magnificent flowers and very delicious fruit. However, the tree only flowered/fruited every sixty or so years. A grandparent in the old country would plant this Quattel tree for their grandchildren, knowing they wouldn't see the flowers, nor taste its fruit, during their lifetime but so their grandkids could. Unfortunately, Petter Quattelbaum didn't bring one across the Atlantic Ocean with him in 1736, and the actual Quattel is now believed to be extinct.

My kinfolk then introduced me to the idea of what they called "planting a Quattel." This is when one does something good for someone else without needing to see the fruits of their labor. All of the Quattlebaums vehemently agreed that the best thing a Quattlebaum could do was to "plant a Quattel." If nothing else, it was cool folklore, and I really dug it. I still do.

By 1997, the Quattlebaum Arkansas numbers were greatly dwindling. The older cousins had passed and distant cousins that rarely saw each other were mostly all that remained. Sadly, the 1997 Quattlebaum Family Reunion was one of the last for the Arkansas branch. Its numbers being less than fifty, it was moved in the mid-1990s to a smaller campground north of Toad Suck. Since it was in a campground, and I dearly loved those kin folk, I decided there was no way I was going to miss it and made it my first stop out of Memphis, Tennessee.

Chapter 59
My Oregon Trail
June 1997

The Quattlebaum reunion was in a campground on a lake near Choctaw, Arkansas. I camped next to my parents for a couple of nights and had a wonderful time feeling like a kid again. I was saddened though by the large amount of kinfolk that had passed. Sometimes absence speaks loudest of all.

While I was there, my dad and uncle made sure to take me to the Quattlebaum Family Cemetery in nearby Bee Branch, Arkansas. My great-great-grandfather, Philip Quattlebaum, had donated some of his farmland to a family trust to make sure there was always land to bury a Quattlebaum there. My dad had an engraved brick with my name on it and wanted me to reserve a spot in the cemetery. It was pretty surreal at the time. In hindsight, I think I chose a good spot. It is beautiful country in that area.

I headed out from Choctaw, Arkansas onward to Oregon, deciding to take the northwest route around the Rockies. It was a new part of America that I really wanted to see. So, I headed north out of Arkansas and then into Missouri, doing 45 to 55 mph on back highways the whole way in my VW disco bus. I took the back roads whenever I could and just started absorbing myself in the Ozark scenery.

I happened upon an overnight stop sometime before dark at a state campground somewhere in Southwestern Missouri. I had just finished setting up my van for the night and was starting to make a campfire when a car pulled up behind me and parked. Two giggling ladies in their late twenties jumped out of the car and into the dwindling sunlight. They were alone and wanted to know where I was from. I answered and continued setting up the fire.

Just as I got the fire lit, I asked what was up with them. They said that they were from the nearby town and were mad at their husbands whom they lived with. They had come out here, one of their favorite places, to blow off some steam. They saw my VW van and thought I was a cute looking hippie.

They then said they had marijuana and LSD that they'd gotten from their husbands, and I said, "yes, please." We spent the rest of the night just lying under the campfire light and watching the stars while sharing intimate stories. It never got sexual. I just wasn't feeling it. I didn't know them, was on LSD, and was in a very peaceful and non-sexual mood. Plus, they had told me they had husbands, so I thought it would have been awkward to hit on them while or after we were having such a wonderful experience.

That morning, just before dawn, they said they wanted to drive over to a viewpoint to watch the sunrise and asked if I wanted to tag along. I politely declined, wanting to get some sleep before getting back on the road again. I wearily crept into my van.

Several hours later, shortly before checkout time, I was awakened by the same giggling ladies rocking the van. I opened the door, and they asked if I wanted to smoke a marijuana joint before I headed out. While we were smoking in the van, they let me know they were surprised I didn't join them for the sunrise. "It was beautiful" they said, followed by one of them saying "I bet you'd never had a blowjob by two married ladies while watching a train at sunrise, have you?" Then they giggled and one said, "you really missed out."

I don't know. Something about the vibe kind of creeped me out, and it did not sound seductive to me at the time. I mean, sure, the blowjob and view would have been great, but something about them was just not adding up to me. I told them I had to hurry up and check out, thanked them for the great time last night, and quickly corralled them out of the van. I drove up to the bathhouse to take a quick shower.

While stepping out of the shower, I heard giggling coming from the bathhouse entrance. Sure enough, one of the ladies was standing in the bathhouse entryway with a towel wrapped around her. She dropped the towel and asked me if I wanted to join her in the lady's bathhouse next door as she walked out and headed over to the other side. Bless her heart.

I was very much tempted, but something still felt off. I trusted my gut and quickly got out of there and back onto the highway. I'm sure they were sweet ladies, but, again, it felt creepy, almost like they did this a lot. I just didn't trust it, nor them, and I quickly left without a really good reason to give myself as to why I hadn't stayed another night at that campground. It was like someone was grabbing me by the ear and telling me, "No Brian, come along, you don't want any of that."

I ended up staying celibate for my entire journey and for several months after. I just really wasn't looking for sexual encounters. That's not what my adventure was about. I don't mean to sound self-righteous to the reader by writing that, it's just not what ended up happening. I didn't seek it, and it didn't seek me except for this one time right out of the gates in Southwestern Missouri.

Chapter 60
Kansas City breakdown
June 1997

On the way to Kansas City, I made a startling discovery while stopping to get smokes at a gas station. My van decided that it didn't want to start. I opened the back hood, couldn't find anything obviously wrong, and sat down on the curb with my head in my hands. I sat there for a good twenty minutes, unsure what to do. I decided to give it another try, and the engine started right up. I drove it to a state campground outside of Kansas City and parked it. It didn't start back up. I didn't get a lot of sleep that night.

When I awoke that morning, my van started right back up again with ease. I drove it straight to a VW dealership in Kansas City. They took a look at it, charged me for a fuel cleaner additive and some other bullshit charges, and said they couldn't find anything wrong with it. They sent me on my way. Traveling north and then turning west at Nebraska, I stopped to get gas and the damned thing wouldn't start up again.

While sitting outside of a hole-in-the-wall gas station somewhere in Nebraska and smoking a cigarette, a car full of hippies pulled up. A few came over to talk to me, and I told them the problem I was having with my van. They said they were going to the Oregon Gathering as well and had space for me if I wanted. I was tempted. I went back to my van, and it started up again this time, so I politely declined.

I had figured it out. The van just needed to rest a while after stopping. Unfortunately, it was going to be awkward at gas stations from there on out. I was motivated to make it work though, so I got back in my van and headed to the next state campground. I remember there being a lot of plains as far as my eyes could see. Just flat farmland and tall grass, with barely a tree in sight.

Chapter 61
Lincoln, Nebraska
June 1997

The next day, I rolled into the beautiful city of Lincoln, Nebraska. It was flat, but there were a lot of trees. Seriously, it was gorgeous. I stopped at a public park downtown and just hung out most of the day with random college students while smoking pot. I loved the vibe, which was odd, seeing that it was Nebraska. Surprised the crap out of me.

I camped at a state campground at a nearby lake that night. While gazing out at the stars, two guys walked up to the camp. They were local college students and wanted to know if I wanted to smoke a joint. They ended up being some really cool dudes. We hung out most of the night just chilling and smoking joints.

I continued heading west through the massive plains and corn fields, determined to get to the national Rainbow Gathering. I enjoyed my brief, yet beautiful, time in Nebraska.

Chapter 62
Windy
June 1997

I continued inching northwest towards Oregon, through Nebraska, and then into Wyoming. There were a lot of plains. When I hit Wyoming, there was also a lot of wind. It was so windy that I had to go 25 mph in my van and hold on for dear life through one stretch. When I did my obligatory thirty-minute stop at a gas station, the attendant laughed when I said something about the wind. He replied, "yep, it's always windy here."

I braved this unseen force of nature and remember staying at a fancy campground because it was my only choice. My van shook all night by the wind, unfortunately not for other reasons. It was two days of wind, and then a big sigh of relief when I hooked into Utah and through Southern Idaho. The wind finally subsided.

Chapter 63
Welcome Home
June 1997

I made it through Idaho unscathed and arrived in Eastern Oregon. Since it was getting close to nightfall, I decided to camp the night and try to find the Rainbow Gathering in the morning. I energetically woke up and set out at first light with the only directions I had been given. It was supposed to be somewhere near Mitchell, Oregon. I don't know if it was in Mitchell or Prineville, but I finally found a large notice board outside a laundromat/general store that was covered with Rainbow Gathering directions. It was very timely.

I followed the directions, and eventually some obvious hippie mobiles, and finally made it to the converted parking lot in the middle of the Ochoco National Forest. I parked, thankful the van made it there, and followed the long string of hippies hiking down a dirt road further into the woods. There were a lot, I mean a lot, of hippies. A lot of school buses too, decorated and painted in some of the most beautiful artwork I had ever seen. One school bus had a sailboat permanently attached to the top of it. A huge freakin' sailboat!

When I made it to the Welcome Gate of the entire encampment, I was greeted with a hug by a hippie with a contagious smile. He boasted out loud "Welcome Home brother!," and I felt true love radiating from him. I didn't know him. He didn't know me. He was just some random dude who wanted to know that he was happy I had made it. I was happy as well. Elated.

Chapter 64
1997 Oregon National Rainbow Gathering
June 1997

When I arrived at the encampment, there were estimated to be around 20,000 or more hippies there. At its pinnacle, the estimate was somewhere around 30,000. That's a lot of people descending on a national forest at once. With twenty or more years of experience doing it, the Rainbow Gathering had a lot of practice on how to handle so many hippies at one time.

There were main areas to the encampment for information, barter/trading, family camping, daycare, medical services, and a main circle. The rest of the encampment was mainly spread out through what were called "camps" and "kitchens."

Camps were small groups of people (some knew each other, others were brand new) that set up an ongoing campfire and coffee/tea service for free to everyone. Most would also serve communal meals throughout the day to feed anyone there. That was their kitchen.

It was all donated and all free. Some were small and only had a tent and a campfire, with one hippie sitting there all day and offering free coffee to the other hippies meandering by. Other camps had multiple kitchens that were sprawling contraptions of tarps, tents, and campfires that would churn out food all night and day.

Since there were hundreds of kitchens spread throughout the encampment, nobody starved. As a conscientious aspiring or hard-core hippie, you were encouraged to give back by volunteering part of your day at a kitchen, vital organization, or main area. There was cohesion among this madness.

Everything for the most part was kept classy, aboveboard, and G-rated by folks. There were lots of families with young children there, so a sense of community and being respectful by not flaunting mature themes was important to most everyone. There was occasional nudity, but that was usually done in good taste with a natural vibe.

It was extremely diverse too. There were religious camps, theological camps, and musical camps of every type. Religion was intermixed and interspersed throughout. Islam, Judaism, Christianity, Rastafarianism, Neo Shamanism, Buddhism, and Hinduism were all present in large numbers. Peace, love, and spirituality were the overriding themes. Some of the religions and theologies even mixed with one another, it was all oh so naughty.

Anywhere a congregation of that size of people, no matter their creed or religion, gets together, then there are going to be some bad actors. I was fortunate enough not to run into any of them during my brief time there. Instead, what I witnessed was that everyone was getting along with everyone else. There was such a sense of peace and community that I just wandered in awe the next day or two doing nothing but wandering from kitchen to kitchen and taking it all in.

I want to unfortunately, and against my own advice, take a second to address a new word that has gotten popular among us called "cultural appropriation." I heard it used once by someone to insult a white-skinned young adult who had dreads. I think we use that word way too much and that it can have a hint of fear and hate when being used. I can certainly understand other cultures not wanting their identity to be misconstrued, but what I don't understand is why we shame people for seeking self-enlightenment by doing what works for them?

I've got a well-known secret to tell you if you don't know it already: there is no standard recipe or answer for you to reach self-enlightenment. Everyone who is able to get there (even if briefly), gets there because of finding out what works for them. For one person, their path to self-enlightenment may come through Christianity, for another, it may come through the belief of a Flying Spaghetti Monster, and for others yet (like me) it comes from a blend of ideas and beliefs. I like to call mine "Taoist Christianity." And here's the kicker, that personal recipe can actually change over time.

Why does it matter so much how someone is able to attain their own self-enlightenment? Shouldn't we be encouraging them to pursue what resonates with them in the moment so they can be the best and brightest version of themselves? I don't know about you, but I personally would love to see more self-enlightened people out there. As long as their beliefs or actions aren't hurting others then please don't hate.

Getting back to my own path toward self-enlightenment, I remember waking up my first morning of the Gathering, opening my small tent on the side of a mountain, and feeling the sunshine seep deep into my soul. It was wonderful. I felt radiantly awash in bliss. A small group of hippies came meandering by and inquired if I wanted to smoke a joint with them. So awesome.

I volunteered for the plumbing crew that first week there. I helped carry and install piping for potable water to different kitchens throughout the encampment. I'm pretty sure I was tripping on acid the entire time. LSD and marijuana were plentiful, and, if you volunteered for the right places, you were given as much as you wanted.

I have a friend that went to the same Gathering (I didn't know him or meet him then). He says that the medical center camp (C.A.L.M.) at one point had to pin a large note to the clothing on his chest that said, "No more LSD 4 me."

For the first couple of days, I couldn't find my friends from Memphis. It was just that big. I eventually found them at a barter circle, and we joyously reunited. I couldn't believe that I'd actually made it. They couldn't believe that I'd actually made it.

My friends had been working for the medical center, C.A.L.M., since they had gotten there a couple of weeks ago. One of them, Apple butter, had gotten giardia by drinking some questionable water his first day or two there and ended up in C.A.L.M. (Center for Alternative Living Medicine). C.A.L.M. was the medical/first-aid hub for the entire encampment.

The volunteer staff at C.A.L.M. ranged from hippie doctors (yes, with professional medical degrees) to massage therapists and energy workers. They treated everything from sprains, minor illnesses, bad trips, and lice to skin infections. They had a variety of methods available to treat the hippie in accordance with the hippie's beliefs.

Apple butter, which was what he went by now, his "Rainbow" name, said that he had stayed at C.A.L.M. and ended up volunteering with them for a couple of weeks. I tagged along with him and got to work for C.A.L.M. doing menial tasks. I quickly made friends. Everyone there was great, and the medical knowledge collected in one place was amazing. That's where I first really learned about alternative healing, and how bad I had been treating my physical body. I absorbed a bunch and learned a lot in that week volunteering for C.A.L.M. It was definitely one of the best places to be. Everyone came through there and constantly gave us donations for volunteering.

My Memphis friend, Apple butter, said that he had gotten his new Rainbow name while hanging out with friends at C.A.L.M.

Apparently, or so the legend goes, Apple butter had never heard of the food called Apple butter. One morning, a nearby kitchen was serving it, and the concoction blew his mind. He would not stop raving about it, so someone decided his Rainbow name was Apple butter. Made sense to me, but it was hard for me to get used to calling him Apple butter. It would be a little while longer before I was given a Rainbow name.

Chapter 65
Ashland, Oregon
July 1997

Two of Apple butter's Rainbow friends from C.A.L.M., Hobbit and Soma, had been there since early May and were pretty much partied out by the end of June. Hobbit was in his mid-twenties and Soma was in his late teens, and they wanted to go back to their base of operations in Southern Oregon. They had a fourteen-year-old kid with them that they wanted to get back to the kid's father's place in Ashland, Oregon. The fourteen-year-old kid had long dreads. He was one of the coolest and brightest kids I'd ever met.

Even though the pinnacle of the Gathering wasn't going to happen until the 4th of July, I felt a strong pull towards Hobbit and Soma and seriously considered driving them to the small town of Ashland. It was getting crowded in the woods, hippies were everywhere, and I wasn't really feeling the thought of a huge circle on the 4th of July. Plus, I hadn't taken a real shower in several weeks. I weighed the choices in my mind and eventually offered to take them to Ashland, Oregon to see what the hype was all about. Apple butter and another friend, who played banjo quite well, tagged along.

We hiked out of camp early that morning, and my van luckily started right up. We headed out. Hobbit sat in the front passenger seat and navigated. He wanted to take me along the backside near Crater Lake, Oregon; instead of driving the interstate. We lazily spent the day driving, smoking, chatting, and enjoying the scenery.

Hobbit would quickly become one of the most fascinating people I've ever had the privilege to meet. He told me, on our ride, that he had been born at a Rainbow Gathering, one of the first. His mom was an elder in the Gathering, and he grew up in Gathering encampments while traveling around the country. She'd passed a couple of years prior. He also didn't have a birth certificate, social security number, or any type of real identification. He was able to somehow obtain a library card.

I would later corroborate Hobbit's story through other elders in the Rainbow Gathering community. He was the real deal, and he was a fount of knowledge that had grown up going from one C.A.L.M. encampment to another, usually filling the time by going to Grateful Dead shows. He had been homeless his entire life. For some reason, he really dug me. We became fast friends. His favorite place was where we were heading, Ashland, Oregon.

We arrived in Ashland later that evening, and I parked my van at the fourteen-year-old kid's dad's place. It was a small apartment inside of a house in downtown Ashland. They had me park in an alley. It was dark, and I had no clue where I was.

We went inside the small apartment and reunited the kid with his dad. He was definitely one of the coolest dads I'd ever met. He took immediate interest in my unhealthy diet and gently schooled me for the next week on eating well. I quickly felt better within a week of following his advice. Hobbit was really good about helping me enforce it. My body finally got the nourishment it so desperately needed.

The dad was making pesto from fresh ingredients he got at one of the local farms he worked at. He gave us all a workshop on how to make wonderful pesto that night while smoking marijuana with us and catching up with his kid's antics over the past month. Soma hiked off to go to his dad's house, and I fell asleep that night in my van feeling extremely calm and serene. I dug the vibe of Ashland already.

That next morning, I awoke to a pleasant surprise when I stepped out of my van. Ashland was a beautiful valley town surrounded by hills and mountains. Hobbit and gang took me on a walking tour of the small, quaint houses with alleys and fruit trees, to the town's largest grocery store (a co-op natural foods store near the quaint houses), to the bagel shop on the tourist strip, and then over to the 93-acre downtown park. It was all within walking distance and not overly bougie. I was in paradise.

There were also hippies everywhere, even with the National Gathering going on. That was no big deal to them. They had community obligations.

One term that I kept hearing used at Rainbow Gatherings when describing normal, American society was "Babylon." If you were living in a town or city, you were living in Babylon. That term really bothered me when I first heard it because there was a hint of hate and fear in it due to my Christian Bible upbringing. However, an elder explained it best to me when they said that there were millions of hippies out there in Babylon who keep goodness in their hearts and do their best to forward society.

Just because we live in Babylon doesn't mean that we have to be Babylonian. It really doesn't matter where we are, only that we keep working towards our own self-enlightenment and do the best we can in society. Some of the best hippies are deeply integrated into "American" societies, trying to promote goodness and kindness and planting their quattels however they can; they're not just out in the woods hugging trees.

Chapter 66
Naked hippies on bikes!
4th of July 1997

I awoke alone in the alley on the 4th of July to Hobbit and gang shaking my van. During our morning smoke session, they filled me in on the day of fun-filled excitement. We were going to see a 4th of July street parade in downtown Ashland and then fireworks at the high school later that night. I was extremely skeptical. I mean, that was something that I could experience in Collierville, right?

We made it in time to get a spot up front for the parade. Even though it was one of the smaller street parades I'd ever seen, it was definitely the most artistic. Everything was art. I mean real art, not just roses glued over a frame. It was glorious. The bike art alone was fantastic.

Towards the end of the parade, when I thought things couldn't get weirder, a long string of naked hippies on decorated bikes went by. Everyone was cheering. I was thinking, "man, never in Collierville, lol."

We went to the high school later that evening to watch the fireworks display. It was most impressive for a small town. I've seen some good Southern fireworks shows, and Ashland gave them a run for their money. It was good stuff. I was in paradise. Definitely one of the best 4th of July's I'd ever had.

Chapter 67
My hippie name
July 1997

I awoke the next morning and made my way to the nearest bagel shop. I met Hobbit while there. He invited some of us dirty hippies to hike over to a friend's van that was also street camping in Ashland to smoke marijuana. About eight of us crammed into the back of the van, and the van's owner packed a glass pipe with some really dank kind bud (that's slang for "good marijuana, man").

After I got a hit of the marijuana flower, I asked him if I could take a gander at the bud. He passed his baggie of greenie goodness over to me, and it was the best stuff I'd ever smelled. Then someone who was hitting the pipe exclaimed "oh no, the pipe is broke" (meaning it was empty), so, since I was holding the weed, I piped up immediately "I can fix it!" The van/pot owner just started cracking up, laughing hilariously. I thought he was going to chastise me for offering to repack the bowl with his weed. Instead, he said, "dude, your Rainbow name is 'Mario' because you fix broken pipes."

Everyone in the van laughed hysterically for at least five minutes after that. My name to them, and the Rainbow/hippie community, was Mario from there on out. I liked it. Not that I had much of a choice; once a name like that sticks, you gotta pretty much own it.

Chapter 68
My first bus
July 1997

That next day, Apple butter and one of his friends decided they wanted to go back to the National Gathering. They convinced me to take them. However, when I tried to start my van, it wouldn't start. The engine was trying to turn, it just wouldn't keep going. Something was seriously wrong with it.

I had my van towed to the nearest VW shop in Ashland (there were several at the time). While I was awaiting a diagnosis, Apple butter and his banjo strumming friend decided they were going to hitch a ride back to the Gathering. We bid our good-byes.

The VW shop owner let me sleep in my van on his lot that night. I hung out with Hobbit and friends in the park the next day and tried not to let it stress me. Man, I was stressed though. I went back to the shop, and the owner had some really bad news for me. The piston seals had blown, and it had damaged the engine, causing it to overheat. The reason why it was locking up on me was something called "vapor lock" and was common on early water-cooled engines. It needed a new engine.

He said I could sleep in it again tonight if I needed, but he wouldn't recommend fixing it. He said, "it's not worth it." I was devastated; I loved my van. I had it towed to a VW dealership in the larger nearby city. The hippie dad in Ashland let me crash on his living room floor. Hobbit was already crashing on the couch.

I got ahold of the larger VW dealer the next day, and they had the same bad news. They could give me a little bit of money for it. Hobbit, Soma, and I hiked and bused our way to the dealership.

While I was cleaning out my van with Hobbit and Soma, I suddenly had a very startling dilemma that I was trying to solve. For protection, a year or so back I had bought a 20 ga. pistol- gripped shotgun. I had it locked (unloaded) and stowed under the back bench seat.

When I pulled it out, Hobbit looked at me and said, "dude, what the fuck?" I told him I had it for protection. He said again, "dude, what the fuck?" Soma then also chimed in for emphasis, "dude, what the fuck?"

Taking a moment to think about it, I realized they were right. I had actually thought about using the same gun to kill myself almost a year ago. What the fuck? I decided to immediately take the shotgun to the nearest pawn shop and sell it. In hindsight, I think that was a wise choice.

Later that night, Hobbit had good news for me. He said one of his life-long hippie friends in Ashland was selling their pristine VW camping bus. He was letting it go for a steal because he needed the cash.

We strolled over to Hobbit's friend's house the next morning. I fell in immediate love with the microbus camper at first sight. Deeply, madly in love. It was a green 1976 VW Westfalia Camper with the pop-up top (slanted), original fridge, stove, and sink still in working condition. The manufacturer's plate on the door said it was built in September 1976. The same month and year I was born. Its engine had been refurbished several months earlier.

The bus ran great. I paid cash and immediately took it to a mechanic. They said that it was in great condition. I was extremely relieved and grateful.

One of the best aspects of the bus in my opinion was that it really was a hippie bus. The interior of the canopy that popped up for a fold-out bed was covered in years and years of beautiful hippie art. Everything from moons and stars, rainbows, mushrooms, and positive affirmations. It had it all.

Hobbit and I drove back and parked it at the house where we were staying. Since I now had two beds in my new ride, one above and one below, Hobbit decided to crash in the bottom one. I chose the top fold-out bed because it was like climbing into my own little tent perched high in a tree. It had a mesh-screened window in the canvas I could stare out of, and the bed was also extremely comfortable, even for my tall, lanky ass.

Chapter 69
The hustle
July 1997

That very next day, Hobbit imparted one of his largest nuggets of knowledge upon me. He wanted to know what my hustle was. I was like, "what?" "My hustle," he said. He explained that he wanted to know what I liked to create that we could barter or sell.

He liked creating wire-wrapped jewelry from beautiful rocks, but his favorite thing was the gems and minerals themselves. He was a rockhound. He made his hustle by making beautiful things out of beautiful rocks. His favorite thing to do was to go to places on the West Coast and hand mine rocks to make into jewelry. He would then sell them at public parks, fairs, rock shops, college campuses, music concerts, and flea markets. That blew my mind.

I, as I was with him, was honest and admitted I didn't have a hustle. I then piped up that my uncle was a lapidarist, and I really enjoyed the silver jewelry he had made for sale at the reunions. Hobbit and I started talking about rocks, and, that day, another rockhound was born.

Over the next few days, we traded a small amount of marijuana for cash in order to buy rocks (the natural kind) and wire from the local Ashland stores. Hobbit then taught me the subtle art of wire-wrapping our specimens. After we made a few, we sold them near the park in Ashland to tourists. We easily made back our money and profited enough to stay alive and keep doing it.

While we were selling our jewelry on the streets of Ashland, Hobbit taught me another cool jewelry skill; how to make hemp braided bracelets and necklaces. People loved them, especially if the wire-wrap was incorporated into them. I learned to make pieces of art that week, an invaluable life skill.

I decided to stay in Ashland for the rest of July and work on my hustle with Hobbit. Soma's dad had a mountain cabin nearby where some of us hippies decided to go camp for a week or so and recharge in nature. Soma's dad was a really cool, banjo strumming, dude. Hobbit had a djembe drum and knew how to play since he was a little kid, so we all had a great time. Later that month, Hobbit convinced me to go up to Portland and sell some of our jewelry at the main Farmer's Market. Soma decided to come along as well.

We made a good bit of cash in Portland, and on the way back stopped at a riverbed that Hobbit knew of where there were some beautiful, polished by the water, agates we could find. We spent two days finding some really good finds, and Soma discovering a love he didn't know about either, rockhounding.

Chapter 70
On the road again
August 1997

On the way home to Ashland, Hobbit, Soma, and I developed an ingenious plan. We were going to start a rockhounding company where we would hand mine and sell gems and minerals. We would travel to different places that both Hobbit and Soma knew about, camp out and collect samples, and then sell them to rock shops. We would also make and sell jewelry along the way.

It sounded like a blast to me, and at least a little sustainable. Plus, I really wasn't ready to leave the West Coast yet, I had barely scratched the surface. I was all in. We decided to name our business, "Jah Rocks" (Jah is short for Jehovah).

Over the next couple of days, Soma spent time with and said bye to his dad while we all prepared. We piled into my VW bus with all our stuff, a few other hippie friends pitching in for gas money for a ride, and headed south to California.

Chapter 71
Northern Cali
August 1997

Our first stop along our new adventure was Mt. Shasta, California. Hobbit and Soma both had friends there, and we stayed the night in the bus at one of their friend's places. Shasta was a beautiful place, but we unfortunately only spent a day and night there. Hobbit and Soma directed me down to Redding, and then we cut over to mine some agates on the way to the Pacific Ocean. We camped at a river spot that Hobbit knew about but only found a few worthwhile agates.

Come morning, I got to glimpse my first sight of the Pacific Ocean. We turned to go south along Highway 1 and stopped in Arcata at a park near the college. We hung out for a day with some other hippy friends we had reconnected with (the National Gathering was pretty much over at this point) and were fairly successful selling our jewelry. Folks seemed to like it.

There were two things I remember most about Arcata: it was very foggy, and I had some of the best marijuana I've ever had from a hippie's outdoor hydro grow. It was a pretty dank town.

From Arcata, we headed slowly south down the Pacific Coast of Northern California. It was foggy the first day there and I could barely see one of the best attractions on the West Coast, the Pacific Ocean. That next morning though, it was clear and sunny, and the Pacific Ocean gleamed its lovely blue.

I was enthralled with the sweeping views of the trees, hills, beaches, and ocean while driving the bus through the curves. The microbus was fun to drive, and we would stop every couple of hours or so to chill, camp, or see what we could dredge up from the beach. I was in heaven on earth.

We unfortunately didn't find much on our rockhounding quest, just a few moonstones, agates, sea glass, and some pretty serpentine. Hobbit knew we shouldn't carve the serpentine (it's bad to inhale the dust), so we ended up chunking it in its own 5-gallon bucket to sell later. Even though we didn't find much, we still had a blast.

We continued down the Highway 1, creeping our way south towards San Francisco. Unfortunately, we realized as the large city loomed into sight that we had made a grave mistake and couldn't find a spot to camp the night, so we had to go across the Golden Gate Bridge in the dark. I was a little bummed by that, but it was still stunning to see, even at night.

The weather was gorgeous, sunny and in the high-70's, as we trailed down the coast to Santa Barbara the next morning. We continued taking our time, stopping and camping along the way. Hobbit also knew of some stellar beach spots that we would chill and/or rockhound at. We still didn't find anything too great, but we did find some nice, smaller pieces we could wire-wrap. I didn't care; I had gotten to hug at least ten Redwood trees. I was in wonderful bliss.

Chapter 72
Southern Cali
August 1997

We eventually turned at Los Angeles and cruised east. Neither Hobbit, nor Soma, wanted to spend any time in the L.A. area. I agreed that the vibe was not what I was looking for either, so we quickly sped (not really, I could barely do 55 mph in my bus) down Highway 10 and wound-up camping in Palm Springs.

It was surprising to me how long in the desert I felt like we were in before getting to Palm Springs. It's nowhere near the Pacific Ocean. I know on the map it looks like it is, but it is a completely different biosphere. It was still cool though. I mostly remember hunkering down in the hot heat with Hobbit and Soma at a downtown coffee shop while enjoying the cool mist put out by their sidewalk awning misters. It was refreshing.

Eastward though we continued. Hobbit had a great spot where we could go mining just across the Arizona border.

Chapter 73
Quartzsite, Arizona
August 1997

We strolled across the California desert in my bus. It was really pretty, and really hot. I remember us stopping along the way to break and it being scorchingly hot everywhere except in the shade of the bus. I gleefully pranced back and forth, between shadow and sun, amazed at the temperature difference.

Shortly after crossing the Arizona border, we came upon our current destination, Quartzsite. I was a little underwhelmed by the size of the town until Hobbit let me know that it really didn't become a bustling place until the winter. That was when tens of thousands of retired rockhound enthusiasts would migrate south and camp in all the camping spots in the town. I then looked around. There were camping spots to hook up to everywhere. The entire town reminded me of an abandoned campground, just urging to be filled again.

We camped the night in Quarzsite and woke up to a beautiful morning in the desert town. Hobbit then directed me down a small highway for a while, further into the beautifully painted desert. A ways out of town, Hobbit had me turn on a small desert road off the highway.

It was really more of a trail across the desert with tire tracks. He then told me to head down the road for about twenty miles. There were no signs. I was like, "dude, are you sure," and he said, "trust me."

So, we meandered for about twenty miles through the desert around gorgeously colored hills. Just when I thought Hobbit might have lured us out here to eat us, we came upon an empty campsite next to a small glimmering hill in the desert. We made camp and then walked the short distance to the hill. As we came closer, I could see glistening veins of quartz running all along the outside of the hill. The entire hill sparkled in the bright sunlight.

We found a couple of good spots that had been previously mined and reinforced and proceeded to chisel away some of the nicest quartz specimens I had ever seen. The rarest thing about it was that a lot of the quartz had a bluish-gray tint to it. There were silver deposits in the quartz that gave it that hue. It was beautiful. We ended up selling most of our pieces later for a decent price.

We camped that night under the stars. When darkness descended, the coolest thing happened at the campsite when the moonlight came shining down. The sand glittered everywhere with quartz crystal points that had been left behind by other miners. It was a magical place that luckily was cordoned off shortly afterward due to fear of overuse.

Chapter 74
Rainbow reunion
August 1997

We didn't stay in Quartzsite but a few days; it was hot during the day and cold at night. Soma typically slept outside in his sleeping bag unless the weather was crappy. One morning he awoke to a scorpion trying to share his sleeping bag with him. Luckily, neither he nor the scorpion were hurt in the misunderstanding. Soma tried to make it a habit not to sleep on the ground in the desert after that.

According to Hobbit, our next destination on this crazy tour was a very small Rainbow Gathering on Northern Arizona federal land. It was where some hippie elders were meeting up after Oregon to discuss next year's national Gathering site, somewhere in Arizona.

This Gathering was very small, maybe 500 hippies at the most, but we still had a blast. I helped Hobbit and Soma set up C.A.L.M., and we camped for the next week. Hobbit, after giving me drum lessons over the past two months, started letting me play his djembe drum at some of the drum circles. I jammed my heart out and traded some jewelry I'd made for my first djembe.

The Gathering only lasted a week. The community elders through voting and debate had quickly decided on a location for the 1998 Rainbow National Gathering on high-desert land they knew of southeast. Impressed with our C.A.L.M. set-up and first-aid knowledge, some of the elders asked us to come help set-up C.A.L.M. at the fall Gathering during Thanksgiving. It was going to be held in a national forest in Southeastern Arizona.

Now, I'm sure the fact that Hobbit having grown-up under the care of most of the elders and knowing them all had a lot to do with it, but I felt important. I had an important, worthwhile thing to do; provide first-aid to hippies in the woods. It was a daunting task, but very fun nonetheless. I was stoked to be able to do it in November, and this gave Hobbit, Soma, and I a really good reason to stay in Arizona for the fall season.

Chapter 75
Flagstaff, Arizona
September 1997

After the small gathering, a lot of us hippies caravanned it over to Flagstaff, Arizona. Hobbit had friends there and knew of several parks where we could sell our wares. It was a beautiful mountain town with lots of kind folk. We spent a week or so just camping and chilling at the gorgeous parks during the day.

Wanting to make a little extra money and stay in a hotel room for a few days (we really needed showers), I decided to visit the local temporary staffing agency. They told me to show up the next day at 6:00 a.m. That next morning, I rode in an Arizona Department of Transportation van with at least eight migrant workers to Winslow, Arizona to dig a large ditch in the hot sun all day. It was brutal, but I made it. The other workers were fun, even though they barely spoke English, and we made the best of the situation. Plus, at lunchtime I got to say I stood on a corner in Winslow, Arizona while walking to a local gas station.

The next day I worked as a forklift operator in a local warehouse. It was a weird transition. I wasn't really digging this temporary day work stuff. We only stayed in a hotel a few nights.

We then decided to go camping outside of Flagstaff and make jewelry for a few days. On the first day in the high-desert woods, I remember sitting in my parked bus and hearing Soma yelling outside for Hobbit and me to come see what he had found. In his hands he held an unbelievably fake-looking mushroom. It was large, at least a foot tall, and had an eight-inch round cap, gloriously covered in bright reddish orange coloring with white spots.

Soma said it was an Amanita muscaria species, very psychedelic, and that we could shroom our asses off if we wanted to. Hobbit piped up. He had serious objections and said that if it wasn't prepared correctly then we could end up with liver failure, blindness, or death. He wasn't willing to risk it.

Soma was convinced that he wanted to try it though and said he knew the proper preparation methods, so he spent the next day or so preparing the mushroom in a large glass jar we had. With Hobbit objecting again the next day, Soma drank some of the potion.

He then offered it to me, I looked over at Hobbit, who had horror in his eyes, and decided that it was probably best to sit this one out. Plus, I couldn't imagine Hobbit having to drive both of us to the hospital if something went wrong.

Soma quickly went into a very intense hallucinogenic state for the next two days in the woods. His trip was mostly positive, and Hobbit and I helped talk him out of any negative thoughts he was having to keep it positive. Just as Hobbit and I were unsure if Soma would ever be sane again, Soma started to come down and crashed. He woke up the next day and said he had met and conquered some inner demons. He was going to try to be nicer and more helpful to society. I didn't know he could get any nicer or more helpful, but he was convinced he could.

One fortuitous afternoon while slinging our wares in a Flagstaff public park, Jah Rocks received its first real commission. Hobbit, Soma, and I were just hanging out on a blanket and making wire-wrapped jewelry with several pieces on display, when a stunningly beautiful lady in probably her mid-to-late thirties walked by with her bubbly nineteen-year-old daughter. As if compelled by force, the daughter knelt right in front of us and started fawning over our pieces. Her mom came over and started fawning over them too.

They sat with us for at least an hour getting to know us and wanting to watch us work. It was a little weird at first until the mom spoke up and said she had a job offer down in Tucson, Arizona for us if we wanted. Apparently, the mom had a lot of money and was enthralled and intertwined with gem and mineral shows and wire-wrapped jewelry.

She said our pieces were some of the best she'd ever seen and could only imagine what our work would be like with higher-quality gems and minerals wrapped in gold wire. Our eyes lit up; we could only dream to work with such materials. She then said, "We can host all three of you at my house in Tucson and pay you really well to use our materials. You can even help us set up and sell the jewelry at some of the gem and mineral shows if you want. I am willing to pay a lot for your time and craftsmanship."

This sounded way too good to be true to us, but we thanked them for their praise and took her business card. The business card looked legit.

Over the next day or so, we struggled with whether to go down to Tucson. Since I'd never been, and there were also some nice places to rockhound along the way, Hobbit, Soma, and I decided to take the trip.

Chapter 76
Tucson, Arizona
September/October 1997

We rode down to Tucson, via Phoenix, and I got to see a lot more of the starkly contrasting and beautifully painted desert and hills of Arizona. We made it to Tucson without incident, but also without a lot of rockhound finds on our tour south. So, running out of money, we decided to give the rich lady a call. She gave us her address and told us to meet her there the following Monday.

In the meantime, we headed up a mountain just outside of Tucson. I was amazed that there was a large mountain just outside the city in the desert. Who knew? It was gorgeous scenery. My favorite moments were when we would drive up or down the curvy mountainous road at sunrise or sunset. One month earlier I had gotten to see sweeping views of the Pacific Ocean around every curve. Now, I got to see the sky lit up in different colors and vibrant hues. Each turn a different scene in the sky. I felt blessed.

We arrived at the house on time that Monday morning. We were very nervous at first, the house was really large and fancy. We also didn't know if we could smoke marijuana while working. We did our best jewelry work while smoking marijuana.

We found out they were cool, quickly worked out all the details that day, and, when we got down to business, we couldn't believe the horde of semi-precious gems and minerals she had available to wire-wrap. She also had several sets of jewelers' tools of every type, easily enough for us, and we sat at her kitchen table that first day wire-wrapping everything from muldavite to picture lace agates to druzy azurite with 14k gold wire.

We made some beautiful pieces. She and her daughter were very pleased and wanted us to do this several days a week for the next month while also occasionally helping them set-up and sell at weekend gem and mineral shows in Tucson and Phoenix. We jumped at the opportunity.

The next two months were spent making wire-wrapped pieces several days a week for them at her house, setting up and selling our pieces at gem shows, and getting paid a lot of money. There were a lot of perks too. Not only did she pay for a lot of our hotel rooms, but she also gave us a lot of high-quality pieces and other materials for us to make into our own jewelry to sell.

On our off time, we had a blast in Tucson. We made some college friends and started hanging out near the University of Arizona campus. Soma even had a girlfriend for a couple of weeks, and we got to crash at her apartment as well. I turned twenty-one later that month and got to see Santana and Rusted Root perform in the desert. It was a fantastic show.

When we weren't hustling at gem and mineral shows, one of our favorite places to set up was the Tucson Flea Market. Vendor's booths were very cheap and plentiful, and it was always crowded on the weekends. We would set up and play drums all day while selling jewelry and taking in the local folk. They seemed to dig us.

It was during this time that I met the nicest and kindest folk that I'd ever met. We got to know a young couple sitting next to us in a booth one day at the flea market. They didn't speak a lot of English, but had some beautiful wares for sale, and really liked our wire-wraps. The wife asked us that night if we wanted to come over for a home-cooked meal, we couldn't refuse.

We followed them over to their tiny house in Tucson, and they proceeded to host Hobbit, Soma, and I to some of the best home cooked Mexican food I'd ever had. They also let us spend the night there. The fact that they had taken us in, complete strangers who were very different from them, was overwhelming to us in their kindness. We were extremely grateful, and I will never forget their loving hospitality extended towards us that night. It was very timely.

Very untimely was the snowstorm we ran into on the way to Flagstaff one night that late October. We were heading there for an upcoming Halloween party. There were about seven of us hippies in the bus, and we were reduced to a crawl on the highway by the snow. I was shocked that it was snowing in October.

Around fifteen miles south of Flagstaff, my VW bus ran out of gas. We sputtered over to the side of the highway. It was the middle of the night, freezing cold, at least a foot of snow on the ground, and traffic was sparse to say the least. Soma and I braved the cold and stood on the side of the road with our thumbs up, hoping someone would stop. About twenty minutes in, one brave soul pulled behind the bus. An older sedan with one occupant.

Soma and I then watched a loomingly large guy get out of his car and lumber up to us. He was a big dude. He also had a huge, inviting smile and asked if we needed help. I told him our situation, that we had five other hippies in the bus freezing their asses off, and we didn't know what to do. Then, surprisingly, he said he'd been to Rainbow Gatherings and now worked in Flagstaff. He amazingly took us all back to his house for the night.

That guy was in for a pleasant surprise when we busted out some of the marijuana we had left from Northern Cali after we arrived at his house and learned he was really cool. It was some good stuff. We had been saving it.

We had a great time that night, warm in his small, but wonderfully cozy, home. That morning, on his way to work, he gave us one of his gas cans and drove us to a gas station near our stranded bus. He was a kind soul.

Chapter 77
Fall Gathering
November 1997

Come early November, we were exhausted. Hobbit, Soma, and I had been hustling our asses off and were looking forward to camping in the woods for a while. We headed east of Tucson to a nearby national forest, Hobbit guided us to the Gathering base camp site, and we set up C.A.L.M. with some other hippies.

Early that evening, just as we had settled in and decided to go visit the main campfire, a hippie came stumbling up to Hobbit, Soma, and I. He was holding out in front of him a white sheet of paper while wearing surgical disposable gloves. He was giggling with overwhelming glee and said, "are you guys the kids that just set up C.A.L.M.?" We said, "yes," and he let us know that he and his buddy made LSD in their converted hippie school bus. The sheet he was holding was just dipped into a fresh batch. He wanted to know if we wanted some of the first given out.

We all three quickly exclaimed "yes, most definitely," and he then tore off a large paper strip and handed it to me. I plopped the strip into my mouth. It had barely touched my tongue before I was tripping one of the smoothest and best acid trips I'd ever taken. I felt overwhelming joy radiating from inside of me and connecting to everyone else's joy who was tripping around me. One by one, I could tell the hippies that had eaten the LSD and those that hadn't yet. I felt instantly connected.

I'm pretty sure all 2,000 or so hippies in the woods were tripping on LSD for the rest of November. I know I was. I don't remember a lot, but I know I had a blast. My new normal for the month was tripping. It was weird, and then it was sane. I just learned to go with it. Somehow, we were able to keep C.A.L.M. going amongst this new insane world we had stumbled into. It was a trip.

I also used that time to improve my hand drum skills. It's something else to be in a circle around the fire with 100 other hand drums, all wielded by enthusiasts, keeping a rhythm while everyone's tripping. It was like the ultimate concert to me, and I was participating. I could tell the other drummers around me would dig it when I would occasionally slide into a solo for a brief second, adding a compliment to the beat. What a thrill!

Thanksgiving came and went in the high-desert mountainous woods. The Fall Gathering wrapped up with a few hippies remaining to camp out the winter and scope out good camping sites for the National Gathering that next summer. Camping the winter there did not sound appealing to us, so we left with the majority. We were invited back next spring to help set up and drove back to Tucson to camp.

Chapter 78
Winter
December 1997

When we arrived back in Tucson, we called our rich lady, and she had some bad news for us. She wasn't going to any other shows until February, so she didn't need our services again until then. It was kind of a shock for us; we thought we would have work lined up through winter. We drove north somewhere and camped with some other hippies also leaving the Fall Gathering.

Hobbit, Soma, and I came to some conclusions that night. First, we didn't have the money to wait it out until February. Second, we didn't really want to spend winter in the cold Arizona desert. Third, we couldn't agree on where to go next. Soma wanted to go east, and Hobbit wanted to spend the winter in Northern California at a hippie farm he knew of.

I was just plain tired. I wanted real shelter and a place to stay for a little bit. An unknown farm sounded tempting to me, but I was also missing home. I had been staying in touch with my parents during the trip by pay phone, and they were encouraging me to come back to their house to stay.

I made up my mind; I was going to go back to Memphis for the winter. Soma wanted to go with me. We painfully split from Hobbit, dividing our jewelry and other wares equally among us. It was a very sad departing.

My mom had told me on the phone that my grandfather (her dad) in Little Rock, Arkansas was wanting me to stop by if I came that way.

So, Soma and I took turns for the next couple of days driving east from Tucson. We turned north once we crossed into New Mexico to try and hit Interstate 40. On the way up, in the middle of the night, I came upon a very awkward situation.

While cruising along at 50 mph in the bus in the dead of night, I saw some lights flashing ahead of me. When I drove closer, the lights were matched with cones and signs that were telling me I had a stop coming up. It then diverted me into a single lane towards a person standing at a booth that I originally took to be a toll. I yelled at Soma to come up front and slowly took the diverted path. There was zero traffic. It was deserted.

I rolled up to the guy standing at the toll booth and realized two very distressing things. First, that was not a tollbooth, it was a guard booth. Second, that guard standing there was in full on soldier gear and held what looked like a fully automatic assault rifle strapped around his chest. Soma and I had just smoked one of our last marijuana joints and the bus reeked. I'm pretty sure I peed a little in my pants.

Slowly coming to a stop, I rolled my window down and said, "hi, how are you doing?" He just looked at me with a deadpan face and said, "driver's license please." He didn't hand it back and told me to turn off the engine. Fuck, I thought, and I'm sure Soma did too, we're going to jail.

The soldier then walked towards the back of my bus. He shined his light on my license plate and picked up the radio. After a moment on the radio, he walked back to my window and handed my license back. He said, "how many of you are there in there?" as he shone his light through the windshield. Soma and I replied, "just us." The soldier then said, "where you headed?", and I replied, "we're going back to Collierville, Tennessee (near Memphis) to see my folks for Christmas. We spent the fall in Tucson."

That soldier sat there for at least ten seconds in dead silence thinking, and then said, "do you have any drugs in your vehicle?" I could tell that he wanted to search us, but I could also tell he kind of believed us when we exclaimed "no!" It was pretty much the truth, all we had was a joint's worth of weed left and nothing else, not even alcohol.

I guess he figured we weren't worth his time and maybe touched by my going home for the holidays story. He told us to proceed and have a Merry Christmas. I booked it the hell out of there for Interstate 40.

We drove through the next day and didn't sleep until we got to Little Rock, Arkansas. I called my grandfather from a pay phone, and he happily invited us over. I introduced him to my hippie friend, Soma, and my grandfather was actually very welcoming to the both of us. My step-grandmother made dinner and invited us to spend the night.

I was relieved. I had been a little nervous that upon seeing my grandpa, a World War 2 veteran and retired welder, he would immediately tell us dirty hippies to leave. However, his youngest son was also a hippie who had committed suicide in the early 1970s. I think by this time in his life, he knew how short and precious time was and how love and connection was what mattered. We four merrily chatted the night away.

Soma and I drove out the next day to Memphis. Soma was excited to see Memphis for the first time, and I was excited to get back to my parents' house. We arrived a couple of days before Christmas, and Soma stayed with me in the house with my mom doting over us with home-cooked meals and love. That Christmas Eve, Soma and I went to the choir concert at the Collierville United Methodist Church. My dad was singing in the choir.

Soma and I sat silently beside my mom during the service, both of us completely sober, and quietly wept. Tears continuously streamed from both mine and Soma's cheeks. They wouldn't stop. Don't worry, they were joyous tears.

It was a beautiful service, and we both felt Spirit in church that night. Soma admitted the next day that it was surprisingly one of the most at peace and in touch with God spiritual moments that he had ever felt. He never thought that was possible in a church. That was saying a lot for him. Seeing that it happened at a Christian church performance, I was pleasantly surprised it happened to me as well.

Chapter 79
The parting (epilogue)
January 1998

I took Soma to my favorite Memphis spots over that next week and also reconnected with some old friends in Collierville. All of a sudden, I could relate to them now on a social level. I guess I'd finally caught up, or they sensed that I was a much happier and well-adjusted person now. Probably a lot of both.

Soma decided that next week he'd seen enough of Memphis and wanted to head south to Florida. He asked me to take him to a popular highway off-ramp in Memphis and leave him there to hitchhike. We tearfully said our goodbyes, and I bid him the best of luck.

For the first time in six months, I was driving alone. I felt lonely. Surprisingly though, I was also happy and very content. I finally felt like a real person and an adult. I headed back to my parents' house, motivated to do what I could to integrate back into society.

I worked my ass off and was monetarily broke, but not broke in spirit, for many years after that. I had some great times with great friends in Memphis for several years and then eventually moved to Oregon. I was finally able to make enough doing something I enjoyed that could support my basic needs. I also became a loving father and contributed the best I could towards society.

I have struggled, as a lot of us do, with depression and failures throughout my life. But I also have a lot of triumphs that make me glad I continued to keep living towards the end of my teen sobriety. My dark time, when suicide would not leave my thoughts.

I try to keep my head held high now wherever I go. I know I am just a quiet hippie, hiding in the shadows. However, I try to contribute the best this hippie can towards making this world a little better. What matters to me most is how many quattels I can plant before I go and not to give up on myself nor let others dictate how I live my life. I know who I am and am genuinely proud of myself. I'm fairly certain that if there is a God, then they are proud of me as well.

If you are a victim of any of the abuses I mention in this book, I beg of you to please reach out to a mental health professional. No matter your age. You are a survivor and loved. Psychology and psychiatry have changed a lot over the past thirty-five years. You don't have to suffer in silence. If you, or someone you know, is going through an emergency crisis, you can reach out to the National Suicide Prevention Lifeline for help at 1-800-273-8255. The National Runaway Safeline at 1-800-786-2929 is another great resource. They are both allies.

I leave you with one of my favorite quotes: "One does not need buildings, money, power, or status to practice the Art of Peace. Heaven is right where you are standing, and that is the place to train."- Morihei Ueshiba, founder of Aikido

It is now time for our journey towards self-enlightenment to continue. Please realize that it's never too late to plant a quattel or two in this world. We definitely could use more of them. Welcome Home! Godspeed and God bless.

SECOND CHANCE, INC.

CLIENT RULES

RULES FOR DAILY LIVING AT HOME OR IN GROUP

1. HONESTY!

2. No newcomers talking to newcomers.

3. Pay attention to the person who is talking.

4. No druggie friends sitting next to druggie friends and no sister/brother sitting next to sister/brother.

5. All medication must be checked out by our medical consultant.

6. If you get sick, report to Staff.

7. There will be no smoking by anyone at any time in the building. No client will be permitted to smoke while on their program or during their follow-up phase.

8. No talking in the bathroom.

9. If you or your newcomer need a drop-off, check with staff 48 hours in advance.

10. No stopping anywhere to and from the program. Fifth Phasers may stop with parents.

11. If you are late, you make up a day. If your newcomer is late, you make up a day for him. If you sign in after 9:00 A.M. daily, you are late!

CONFIDENTIALITY

12. WHAT YOU SEE HERE, WHAT YOU HEAR HERE, WHAT YOU DO HERE, REMAINS HERE!!

13. No breaking anyone's anonymity.

14. No talking behind anyone's back.

15. No telling your parents your first phase host parents' name, telephone number, or address.

-1-

DRESS RULES

16. Guys wear shirts, girls wear bras, everyone wears socks.

17. Everyone must wear shoes with backs. No boots in group.

18. No wearing of any jewelry, no make-up the entire time of your program; watches may be worn on Third Phase.

19. No overalls, t-shirts or shirts with writing. No patches on clothing. No leather or jean jackets.

20. No belts for first phasers.

OPEN MEETING

21. No passing anything during Open Meeting.

22. No cameras, tape recorders, or radios. No writing anything during Open Meeting.

23. No eye games with parent during Open Meetings.

24. Everyone attends Open Meeting on Friday Night.

25. Stand up when parent(s) stand up.

26. No talking out to parents except for "I Love You."

27. Open Meeting Introduction: Name, age, drugs, how long you used drugs, how long in the program, past--present--future.

28. No asking parents for wants and needs during TALK.

29. No asking Fifth Phasers questions during Open Meeting.

30. If you are an oldcomer and have a brother or sister who earns TALK, you do not sit in on the TALK.

COMMUNICATION

31. Permissions must first be okayed by parents and then
     okayed by Staff and requested 72 hours in advance. The
     only permissions Second Phasers are allowed to put in
     for are doctor's appointments. (Emergency only)

32. Follow chain of command.

33. Report all stashes. (e.g. drugs or stolen articles)

34. If you notice anyone who plans to leave the program
     without permission, report it to staff.

35. Check out your own drop-offs and permissions.

36. Report any suspicious looking characters.

37. No making or receiving phone calls on Phase I, II, or
     III, except for out of town clients who may call their
     parents on Second and Third phase following phone
     therapy procedures. Fourth Phasers may make and re-
     ceive phone calls and letters.

38. No radio, television or reading on First, Second and
     Third Phase. (Third Phasers may read school related
     material; Second Phasers may read the Bible and the
     Big Book of A. A.)

39. No playing off.

OTHER IMPORTANT RULES

40. No dating while you are on your program or on six
     month follow-up.

41. No hitchhiking or picking up hitchhikers.

42. No borrowing.

43. No animals allowed in the building.

44. No old druggie friends or druggie hangouts.

45. Unless otherwise specified by Staff, bedtime while on
     phases is 11:00 P.M.

46. No rock and country music while you are in your phases
     or six month follow-up.

47. No loitering or talking in the parking lot.

48. Knock on all doors before entering.

49. No going outside on First or Second Phase.

50. No writing M.I.'s or going to sleep with the radio or T. V. on.

51. Hang on tight to Newcomers by the belt loop.

52. Go over Newcomers M.I. at night-time, not in the morning.

53. A permission must be submitted and approved before returning to school or work.

54. While on third phase a yard permission may be submitted 72 hours in advance for yardwork only.

55. On third phase a permission may be submitted to go to the doctor, dentist, or for a haircut.

56. On third, fourth, or fifth phase you may not have more than $5 in group.

57. On first phase moral inventories are written on the past for the first two months and then 50% on the past and 50% on the present.

58. On second phase moral inventories are written 50% on the past and 50% on the present.

59. On third phase moral inventories are written primarily on the present.

60. On fourth and fifth phase moral inventories are written on the present.

61. On fourth phase a driving permission may be submitted.

62. On fourth phase you may go into the yard without a written permission and without your parents.

63. On fourth or fifth phase no watching PG-13,R, or non-rated movies.

64. On fourth phase you may submit a permission to play a musical instrument.

65. On fifth phase you may submit a pretraining resume.

66. On your day off you may call the building to see if you need to return the building for dismissal.

SCHOOL RULES

67. There is to be no therapy at school.

68. Clients may discuss challenges at school on a
    superficial level.

69. Two program druggie friends may be together
    only if there is a third party present, even if the
    third party is another program druggie friend.

70. Males and females may associate but not on a one to one
    basis.

71. Major challenges at school should be dealt with by
    calling a staff member.

TELEPHONE THERAPY

Telephone Therapy - Get three oldcomers telephone
numbers and a Junior Staff Members telephone number. It
is your responsibility to get these telephone numbers before
going into Second Phase.

TEMPORARY HOME/HOST HOME RULES AND REGULATIONS

The temporary home is a place for the children to think
about themselves with the help of their oldcomer. Time
should be spent in the writing of a Moral Inventory which
is another tool to help them get to know themselves. Their
oldcomer is responsible for them, but the parents of the
oldcomer are in charge of the household. This should be
remembered. Parents shall in no way punish host clients.

Other standards for the temporary home are assurances of
fire, safety, sanitary conditions, adequate provisions of
food, adequate sleeping accommodations, and contact with
the oldcomer's family.

Snacks may be given at night, but are not required.
Suggestions for snacks include fresh fruit, raw vegtables,
and popcorn. Each child should be encouraged to drink
plenty of water while at the temporary host home.